VOYAGES OF
THE CELTIC SAINTS

VOYAGES OF
THE CELTIC SAINTS

GRAHAM PANES

GRAHAM PANES

Graham Panes was born in Gwent, South Wales, into a diverse family which included miners, farmers, doctors, sailors and lay preachers. He now lives in Conwy, North Wales. After education in Glamorgan and University of London, where he took a degree in Geology, his work as a Chartered Loss Adjuster took him to all parts of the United Kingdom and Ireland, and he has travelled extensively through Europe, Australia and New Zealand, South America, China and Zimbabwe. He has been sailing boats from an early age and is an experienced yachtsman, holding Yachtmaster (Offshore) and Cruising Instructor Certificates. His own voyaging around the Celtic coastline of the British Isles, and familiarity with the locations associated with the Celtic Saints, has provided the inspiration for this book.

He is the author of a number of contributions to sailing publications.

© Text: Graham Panes

ISBN: 978-1-84527-146-6

Published with the financial support
of the Welsh Books Council

Cover image: Two monks praying at Tynemouth British Library
Cover design: Sian Parri

Published in November 2007
by Gwasg Carreg Gwalch,
12 Iard yr Orsaf, Llanrwst, Wales LL26 0EH
☎ 01492 642031   🖷 01492 641502
✆ books@carreg-gwalch.co.uk   Website: www.carreg-gwalch.co.uk

Contents

Notes on terms

Celtic   Term for the people who spoke Celtic
                  languages

Brythonic   The branch of the Celtic language spoken in
                  Wales, Cornwall and Brittany.

Goedilic   The branch of the Celtic language spoken
                  in Ireland, Scotland and the Isle of Man

Brythons   The Celtic people of Southern Britain
                  (mainly Roman Britain) from 500 B.C.
                  onwards and the forefathers of the Welsh,
                  Cornish and Breton nations

Introduction

Who were the Celtic Saints?

The Celtic saints were restless, energetic, adventurous people who thrived in the rough and tumble, chaotic, often dangerous world of post-Roman Britain. The men were the alpha males of their day, influencing kings and common people, shaping the lives and destinies of individuals and countries. They exercised authority, sometimes through great teaching monasteries, sometimes from preaching on a windswept headland, sometimes leading an army on the field of battle.

They were the most educated men and women of their time, not only in the pious and devout world of their calling but also at the leading edge of knowledge of astronomy, mathematics, geography, medicine and agricultural practices. Many of them had the advantage of noble birth or support from wealthy families, and so had financial and often political power to assist them in their endeavours. They travelled widely through the Celtic areas of Ireland, Scotland, Wales, Cornwall, Brittany and beyond. Journeys to the Mediterranean, Egypt and Palestine did not daunt them. They voyaged by sea and river.

Not all of their travels were in direct pursuit of their calling. Whilst they were required to attend distant monasteries to teach, or to complete their own education, or wander to remote pagan areas in search of converts, they also travelled for the same range of reasons that compel all people.

Columba, for example, sailed from Howth to the former druid island of Iona to seek solitude and a pure life, finding it necessary to expel all women, cows and snakes in order to achieve this. St Tysilio fled from Church Island (Ynys Tysilio) in the Menai Strait to Brittany to escape a Saxon invasion or, possibly, unwelcome demands from the widow of his brother. Teilo, after travelling with St David (Dewi Sant) from Wales to Jerusalem, left Wales again to settle in

Cornwall. From here he made a hasty departure to Brittany to escape a yellow plague epidemic that was sweeping through Britain. He later returned to lead an army of Britons, which defeated an invading pagan army of Angles.

Brendan of Clonfort, often known as Brendan the Navigator, was an adventurer who set off with twelve companion monks from the southwest of Ireland in a boat made of leather hides stretched over an ash frame, to sail far into the North Atlantic, making a passage which included landing at the Hebrides, Orkneys, Faeroes, Iceland and Labrador.

Pelagius, who is referred to scathingly by St Jerome as 'that fat hound full of Scotch porridge' voyaged from Wales to Rome, Carthage and Alexandria, as well as preaching what was condemned as heresy throughout Britain and Ireland. Fidelis is reported to have sailed down the Nile and seen 'the Barns of Joseph' (the pyramids).

Illtud took a convoy of grain ships from southern Wales to Brittany to relieve a famine.

Columbanus was constantly striving to widen the influence of the Celtic Church in Europe and so voyaged not only across the seas to the French Atlantic coast, but along the major rivers such as the Loire, the Saone, the Mosel, and up the Rhine as far as Lake Constance in Switzerland. He later went on to Bobbio in Italy. As well as founding monasteries, he has also left us his famous rowing song, many poems, letters and accounts.

Women also played a prominent role in the Celtic Church, many leading dynamic and influential lives which were greatly venerated. St Keyne, for example, was born in southern Wales and rejected all suitors to become a nun. After her religious education she voyaged in a coracle to Cornwall to undertake missionary work, and founded a cell where the village of St Keyne now stands. Keyne also trekked across Cornwall to visit St Cadog at St Michael's Mount, before sailing back to Wales, where she founded a number of churches.

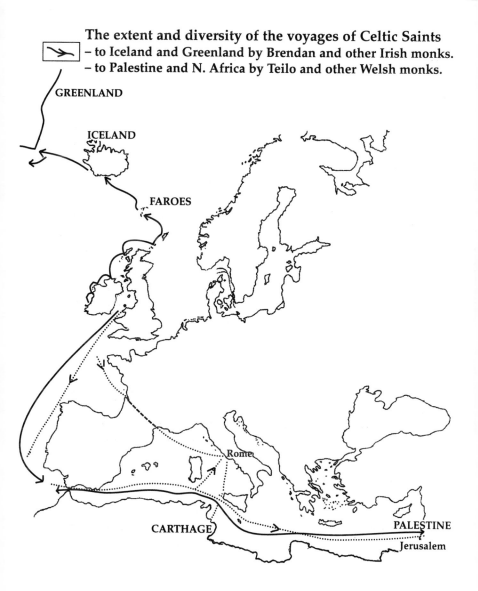

The extent and diversity of the voyages of Celtic Saints
- to Iceland and Greenland by Brendan and other Irish monks.
- to Palestine and N. Africa by Teilo and other Welsh monks.

GREENLAND

ICELAND

FAROES

Rome

CARTHAGE

PALESTINE

Jerusalem

Voyages of Welsh Saints to Rome, Jerusalem, Carthage
David, Seiriol, Teilo, Pelagius and others

Another prominent woman priest was St Kywere, born in south-western Wales, who also sailed across the Bristol Channel to Cornwall where she founded a nunnery at St Kew, and had a large following. Kywere is also believed to have voyaged across the Irish Sea to the Wicklow area of southern Ireland.

St Helen, also known as Elen Luyddoc, was a native of Caernarfon and moved with her husband Magnus Maximus (Macsen Wledig), to Trier in Gaul. Magnus was later murdered in Italy, and Helen then travelled to Tours before returning to northern Wales. Such was her reputation that she was enthusiastically welcomed and became renowned for her kindness and charity. She also had a very strong and commanding will and protected her community by leading an army when the area was threatened by pagan invaders. She also improved communications by building roads, the most famous of which is Sarn Helen, a route-way which can still be traced across Wales from Conwy to Glamorgan.

These are just a few of the Celtic saints who made their mark on early middle ages history, and have left lasting epitaphs in countries throughout Europe.

The Celtic saints were the most venerated of a small number of energetic and influential priests of the Celtic Church, which formed part of the early Christian Church in Britain and Ireland. They rose to prominence during the post-Roman period of the fourth to sixth centuries, a dangerous and chaotic period in western Europe, particularly so in Britain after the withdrawal of the Roman Legions in 410 AD. The Celtic saints were monks, nuns, bishops, abbots and abbesses engaged in the teaching, pastoral and missionary activities of the Celtic Church.

The monk and historian Gildas was the first to use the term 'sancti' to describe the early Christian missionaries who established their churches in Celtic Britain and Gaul. 'Sancti' later became translated as 'saints' and was applied to prominent Christian monks and nuns who acquired a cult status within Celtic Britain, Ireland and France. Many of the

Celtic saints are not officially recognised as saints by the Roman Church. They have not been canonised, but the title has been bestowed upon them by cult followers, or by historians intending to promote their virtue, piety and popularity. During the course of missionary work amongst their fellow Celts and also in conversion of pagan communities, the saints invariably established cults that reflected their particular aestheticism and practices.

The saints were active throughout the early middle ages, but their influence waned in the late seventh century when the Roman Church became the uniform Christian authority in Britain.

What was a Celtic Saint?

Many of the saints were adventurous travellers over great distances, frequently making long sea-going voyages in small craft over dangerous seaways. To appreciate why they undertook such arduous voyages and exposed themselves to such constant danger, it is necessary to look more closely at what motivated them.

The Celtic saints actually existed – they are not fictional characters, even though some incredible and miraculous exploits are attributed to them. Whilst some of these are best understood in terms of folklore, it is important to appreciate that early Celtic culture was not a literary but an oral one, and its history was carried down through generations in stories passed on by word of mouth. In some events a process may have taken place that might have been described in a magical or supernatural way, but these legendary attributes should not be allowed to detract from the historical reality of the saint's existence. It is often difficult to verify the activities of individual saints, and indeed there is in many cases a lack of clarity or considerable confusion over the identity, parentage, birthplace or even age of individual saints. Nevertheless there is no doubt of their impact as a cohesive body and, in some cases, outstanding influence as individuals. The saints were a stalwart force in

11

fighting a reversion to paganism in the Romano-Celtic lands in Britain and in Gaul. They generated a resurgence of Christian faith and played a monumental role in maintaining the character of Celtic heritage in what was becoming a geographically fragmented society.

A picture of the Age of the Saints can be constructed by carefully considering all of the various sources of information, including archaeological remains, geographical evidence of place-names, written records, linguistic patterns of the period, cultural evidence, and oral tradition. All sources must be treated with care – archaeological evidence, for example, can be useful in terms of dating, but may perhaps be debateable in some instances with regard to interpretation. Geographical evidence, such as location and names of present-day settlements, can be particularly useful in establishing cultural and historical factors. In this context the use and distribution of language indicates the movement of cultural groups, often indicated in place-names.

Written records, whether in manuscripts or on inscribed stones, can be more informative, particularly inscribed stones which are usually contemporaneous with the time to which they refer. Manuscripts can be misleading as they are usually written several hundred years after the event being recorded, and so after the event has been in oral circulation for several generations. Finally, there is folklore and oral tradition – never an entirely reliable source but sometimes an encouraging support for harder but incomplete evidence from other fields.

The names of many of the Celtic saints are familiar to us today for a number of reasons. Some are in common usage as patron saints of present-day regions or countries such as Patrick for Ireland, David for Wales and Samson of Brittany – whilst others are patrons of purely local influence, perhaps of small towns and villages. Some Celtic saints are commemorated as patrons – not just of regions, but of particular activities or emotions, such as the hospice charity bearing Kentigern's name, or St Dwynwen, patron saint of lovers. Almost all of the Celtic saints are honoured and commemorated by a Saint's day – for example Patrick on 17 March, and Dewi/David on the 1 March.

Place-names Associated with Saints

There is a prolific use of the names of Celtic saints to identify geographical features, such as islands, coves, bays, villages, towns and even cities, not only throughout the British Isles but also in western Europe. In many cases the designation is a simple prefix of 'Saint' – as found for example at St Mellons, St Austell, St Athan or St Albans. There are also the more ancient forms of place-names designated by the prefix of 'Llan' in Wales, 'Kil' or 'Cil' in Ireland and Scotland, 'Loc' in Brittany and 'Keills' in the Isle of Man. Originally the Welsh word 'llan' referred to an enclosure, which could be specific as is the case in 'gwinllan' – vineyard; 'perllan' – orchard; 'corlan' – sheepfold; and 'llannerch' – clearing or open space. 'Llan' in the context of a holy or Christian enclosure was at one time a secondary usage, and although it became the predominant usage it should not be assumed that all 'llans' have a religious context. Nor can it be assumed that when a religious context is established, that every 'llan' connotation refers to a Celtic saint, for in Norman and medieval times many churches that were originally dedicated to Celtic saints were re-dedicated to Biblical saints, which is why there are many Llanfair (St Mary) and Llanfihangel (St Michael) dedications in Wales.

Archaeological Evidence of Saints – Inscribed Stones

Archaeological remains provide strong evidence of developments during the Age of the Saints. As the story of the Celtic saints unfolds, the importance of the western sea routes in the maintenance and development of Christianity along the Atlantic seaboard of western Europe emerges. The archaeological evidence dating from the Age of the Saints includes the identified remains of monasteries, cells,

13

churches, chapels, wells, enclosures, Christian burial sites, and inscribed standing stones throughout the former Celtic lands of Britain, Ireland, Galicia and Gaul.

There are many examples of upright standing stones inscribed with lettering and numerals dating from the Roman and post-Roman period of Britain, particularly in the western areas. These provide clear evidence of the sea routes taken by saints or missionaries who carried the Celtic or Romano-Celtic message of Christianity across regional borders.

The earliest groups of inscribed stones are from the fifth and sixth centuries, and are of Roman origin. They are distributed in north-western and south-western Wales, and inscribed in Latin. The style of writing and cultural references establish that the 'authors' or 'patrons' of these stones originated in the Lyons and Vienne areas of Gaul, indicating that Christianity was re-introduced to western Wales from France by missionaries travelling the western sea routes who were still imbued with Roman culture. The stones can often be dated as accurately as their origin can be traced – for example, the inscriptions on a stone at Penmachno in the Conwy valley records that it was set up at the time of Justinius the Consul. Justinius is known to have been a Roman Consul in 540 AD but on the European mainland the use of his name is only found in the Lyons area. There are no inscribed stones of this era in south-eastern Wales or in the eastern borderlands previously under Roman occupation, which therefore indicates that this was a new wave or resurgence of Christian influence stemming from the strong monastic movement within the church in Gaul.

The distribution of the fifth and sixth century Romano-Gallic stones indicates that missionaries landed on the western shores of Britain and then travelled eastwards inland along the old Roman roads, as illustrated by the group of standing stones of this era in the Brecon region of south-eastern Wales.

Later groups of inscribed stones are significant not just

INSCRIBED STONES IN WALES 400 - 700

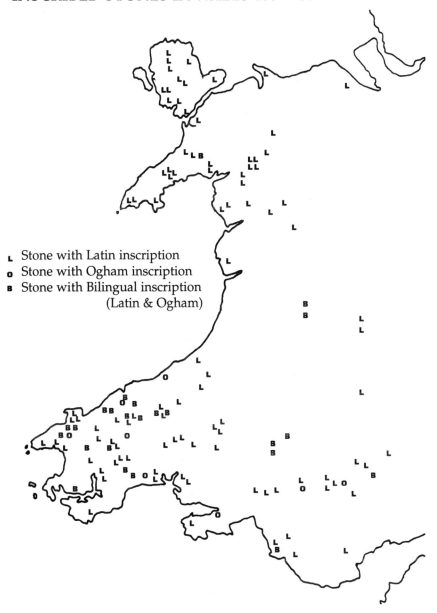

L Stone with Latin inscription
o Stone with Ogham inscription
B Stone with Bilingual inscription
       (Latin & Ogham)

because of their location or the message they carry, but because of the language in which the message is inscribed. The oldest alphabet found on the British standing stones is Ogham, which originated in Ireland. These stones demonstrate that during the fifth century Irish monks were making inroads into western Britain, after crossing the Irish Sea in small sailing boats.

The Ogham alphabet consists of inscribed lines carved into stones. These Ogham-inscribed stones are found not only throughout Ireland, the western parts of Scotland, southern Wales and Cornwall, but as far away as the coast of Labrador, where early Irish monks set up retreats. The location of the Ogham-inscribed stones is clear evidence of the influence of Irish saints on their Celtic neighbours in the post-Roman period, although, significantly, there are no Ogham stones in northern Wales. The Irish and Gallo/Romano influences were at times contemporary with one another and in south-western Wales there are bilingual stones inscribed in both Latin and Ogham, which indicates significant cultural interactions during the early middle ages.

In northern Wales there are only Latin-inscribed stones, and these bear references and designs that reflect a Romano-Christian influence originating in Gaul. There is a wider variety in southern Wales, where some stones have Latin inscriptions that are clearly the work of a Romano-British influence emanating from within the British Isles, while others are Gallo/Romano or Ogham.

Literary Evidence of Celtic Saints

The manuscript *De Excidio Britanniae* (The Destruction of Britain) which was written by Gildas in 540 AD, is an important account of the events of his time. Gildas was not the only Celtic monk whose written record survives, for there are also, for example, the writings of Patrick, who self-deprecatingly apologises for his poor Latin, and the many letters of the Irish monk Columbanus, who wrote frequently

OGHAM INSCRIBED STONES 400-700

to the Pope – not only about his own concerns but also referring to other saints of his era. The Irish *Book of Lismore* records activities of many saints, as do many other works of the Irish monasteries.

Some of the manuscripts dealing with the Celtic saints are accounts of individual saint's lives, such as the *The Life of Columba*, written by Saint Adomnan some two hundred years after his death and *The Life of Saint Samson*, written in France some three hundred years after the saint's death. The Lives of individual saints often include references to other saints with whom they had been associated. Adomnan's work includes references to Cormac, and in *The Life of Saint Samson* the author refers, amongst others, to Samson's teacher, Illtud, 'the most learned of the Britons', who founded at Llanilltud Fawr in southern Wales one of the greatest teaching monasteries in the British Isles.

As well as the manuscripts of Gildas and Bede and letters of Patrick and Columbanus there were countless monks in Wales, Ireland, Scotland, France and Germany who recorded lives of the saints, albeit sometimes several hundred years after their deaths. While detailed and authoritative historical records of the time are relatively sparse, there is enough material about many of the Celtic saints to allow a picture of their lives, and their contribution to Celtic social and religious development to emerge.

Chapter 1

The Celtic Saints

Celtic Languages

The linguistic evidence of place-names in Britain indicates that Celtic peoples had reached the British Isles long before the first historical references to the islands. Between 750 and 500 BC Celtic culture and language had spread into southern Britain as far as Scotland, and Ireland had also received its first Celtic people before 500 BC. The Belgae, Bretons, Gauls, Britons, Irish and Welsh were Celtic people who had a strong cultural identity, and were also unified by speaking a Celtic language for at least five hundred years before the Roman invasion of Britain. The eighth-century monk and historian, Nennius, wrote that at the time of the Roman invasion of Britain: 'The Britons the Brythonic branch of the Celtic tribes filled the whole island with their children from the Sea of Ictus to the Sea of Orcs' [from the Solent to the Pentland Firth].

Linguists have determined that there were two primary Celtic languages used in the British Isles, identified as P Celtic, spoken by the Brythonic Celts of Britain's mainland, and Q Celtic, spoken by the Goedelic Celts who occupied Ireland and later colonised the Scottish highlands and islands. Brythonic later developed as very early Welsh and the Goedelic language became very early Gaelic.

These languages continued to be used in areas of Britain – the Romans did not have a policy of imposing Latin over the native languages. In Roman times even the Celtic aristocracy who accepted 'Romanisation' in areas of Britain's south coast continued to speak Welsh, and the language was only eradicated when the region became Saxon-held in post-Roman times.

Further evidence that a Celtic language was spoken throughout Britain is derived from an analysis of place-names which are essentially P Celtic 'Welsh' in origin, and which are found throughout Scotland, and originated some 2,000-2,500 years ago. The names of Scotland's three major cities – Aberdeen, Glasgow and Edinburgh – are of Welsh origin, as are the areas known as Lanarkshire, Renfrewshire, Perthshire, Dumfriesshire, the Lothians and many more.

The earliest poetry composed in Scotland 'Y Gododdin' was written in Welsh in the seventh century by the Welsh poet Aneirin to celebrate the heroism of the Brythonic Gododdin tribe on their defeat by a Saxon army at the battle of Catraeth. The precise location of Catraeth is not known but is likely to have been modern-day Catterick. Welsh was still spoken south of the Forth-Clyde line in Ayrshire, Lanarkshire Renfrewshire and the Central Borders of Scotland up to the thirteenth and fourteenth centuries – the areas of the 'Strathclyde Brythons' or the 'Strathclyde Welsh'. Sharing a common language was a significant factor in enabling Celtic regions and particularly Celtic saints to maintain contact despite the divisive effect of later invasions by Romans, then Saxons and other pagan tribes. The former widespread usage of a Celtic language throughout Britain was a significant factor in binding together Celtic Christian communities during the Age of the Saints.

What do we mean by Celtic?

There are wide ranging popular understandings of what 'Celtic' means. There is a general awareness that within the British Isles today there are areas considered to be predominantly 'Celtic', particularly Ireland, Scotland, Wales, The Isle of Man, Cornwall and parts of western England such as Cumbria. The same designation is often given to the inhabitants of Brittany, parts of northern Spain and northern

Portugal. There is an understanding that all of these areas share a common cultural affinity going back to ancient times which is different to that of other parts of the population within the same country.

There is, however, a danger in being too specific in trying to locate present-day affinities in any single racial origin.

Although Celtic people occupied most of Europe and had a distinct culture, it is not known from where they had originated – their ethnic origin is a matter of supposition. They were not unified in a political sense and there were significant cultural differences between various groups.

However, as an ethnic group, the Celts were very well known by the Greeks, who, in the fifth and sixth centuries BC referred to them as 'Keltoi', and by the Romans, who later referred to them as the Gauls in France and the Britons, or the Brythons, in the British Isles.

The Celtic tribes who occupied the British Isles and western Europe before the expansion of the Roman Empire shared a common language and social structure. They had a clear appreciation of what cultural group they belonged to within the context of a tribal structure. This is very important in appreciating why, despite the divisive and isolationist effects of the successive invasions of Romans, then Saxons, Angles, Jutes and other Germanic tribes, regions which retained their Celtic identity continued to maintain trading and cultural links, even though political and geographical barriers then separated them. The explanation of the survival of these 'cultural provinces' is highlighted in an observation of Professor Jones that was as applicable to the Age of the Saints as it is to present-day people of Celtic origin: 'For ethnic identity what matters most is what group we think we belong to.'

An example of this was the reaction of the Celtic saint, Beuno, to hearing English spoken on the far bank of the river Severn – he immediately left the area, leading his followers along the old Roman road to set up a new community in north-western Wales. Despite four hundred years of Roman

TRIBAL AREAS OF BRITISH ISLES
Early 2nd Century

Picts

Votadini

Novantae

Northern
Ui Neill

Carvetii

Ulaidh

Nagnate

Brigantes

Southern
Ui Neill

Setantii

Auteini

Fir
Domnann

Deceangli

Coritani

Iceni

Ordovicies
Cornovii

Brigantes Deisi

Catevellauni
Trinovantes

Erainn

Demetae

Silures

Dobunni

Belgae

Cantiaci

Durotriges

Regini

Dumnonii

occupation of Britain, St Beuno and his followers considered themselves to be Celts and spoke a Celtic language. The unwelcome snatches of English conversation heard over the river signified the presence of Saxons – a totally incompatible cultural group as far as St Beuno was concerned. Similarly, when saints such as Teilo and Tysilio were forced to flee their homeland in Wales by Saxon and Angle invaders they knew they would find safety and welcome in the former Celtic area of Gaul.

The Celts were a well-organised and diverse society, with many specialists, such as traders, shipbuilders, warriors, farmers, miners and skilled metal workers. They had their own active trade routes throughout northern Europe and the Mediterranean, exchanging grain, copper, lead, gold and silver and manufactured goods for wine, olive oil and pottery, and carrying trading goods on their own ships from Ireland and Britain to northern Europe, Gaul and Galicia.

Celtic allegiances

During the Age of the Saints there were networks of Celtic regional allegiances, which were sometimes geographically distant from one another, but which contributed to the infrastructure necessary to support voyages along the western sea routes. These allegiances were the foundations upon which the Celtic saints could develop their work in the society that evolved in the chaotic and turbulent aftermath of Roman withdrawal from Britain and Gaul. The regional allegiances were built upon the remnants of Celtic tribal structure, which had retained factors such as a common language and culture underpinning the cohesive and uniform nature of Celtic Europe, particularly the British Isles, before the divisive effect of the Roman invasion.

In pre-Roman times there were no political borders as there are today, but there were significant, clearly defined territorial regions occupied by Celtic tribes. The society was tribal and warrior-based and whilst there were extensive trading links, tribal territory and assets – whether minerals, agricultural land or trading ports – were fiercely guarded. This tribal culture existed throughout western Europe.

In the central and eastern areas of Britain the tribes were eventually subjugated by the Roman occupation, and the areas over which they had previously ruled were completely Romanised, both administratively and culturally. They evolved into a society which became urbanised along Roman social patterns, with large estates and villas.

In contrast, the Roman occupation of the northern and western areas of Britain was primarily a military one, established to protect the sources of valuable minerals such as gold, tin, copper and lead, and also to control tribes most resistant to colonisation. This is indicated in these areas by the archaeological remains of legionary fortresses and military roads, rather than the prevalence of villas or municipal centres of the Romanised areas of central and southern lowland Britain.

The new Brythonic Kingdoms of the post Roman Period

As the Roman Legions continued their march to the west and north they drove a wedge between Celtic tribes that had previously enjoyed uninterrupted trading and cultural exchange, particularly between Wales and southern Scotland. New boundaries were imposed, such as Hadrian's Wall, which was to cut off the north Brythonic tribes for three hundred years. Whilst these tribal contacts were disrupted and made difficult or perhaps even dangerous to maintain, they were not lost. The cultural changes brought by the invaders were not readily adopted in these isolated areas, and the Celtic languages and customs survived, keeping open the cultural and historical links which in later centuries facilitated the movement of large influential groups of Celtic people such as the family of Cunedda, a Gododdin chieftain who moved from central Scotland to northern and central Wales at the end of the fourth century. These are examples of the long-standing pre-Roman Celtic regional affinities that enabled the Celtic saints to travel widely with the knowledge and confidence that they would be met by a people with whom they shared centuries of historical and cultural relationships.

The Roman occupation of central Britain, therefore, had the effect of driving a cultural wedge between the remaining strongly Celtic tribal areas of the west, the north and the southwest, as the former overland routes they used for trade and cultural exchanges were now through Roman occupied areas. Nevertheless, the people of these remaining, fragmented Celtic areas maintained contact with each other by voyaging along the well-established sea routes along the western coast of Britain.

One beneficial result of the Roman authority was a period of stability in Britain, even for the remaining Celtic tribal areas, which evolved into larger kingdoms or principalities as an aristocracy developed.

The withdrawal of the Roman legions in the later part of the fourth century, by which time Christianity was established in Britain, was not an opportunity for a resurgence of pagan Celtic society. In many respects the plight of the Britons became much worse as Britain was invaded from the east by successive waves of Germanic tribes, firstly the Saxons and then other groups. These invaders not only overran the formerly Romanised areas of central and southern Britain, but also attacked the western Celtic areas.

By the sixth century some of these formerly Celtic tribal areas, which had in the meantime evolved into larger British principalities or kingdoms, had been defeated by established Saxon kingdoms such as Mercia and Northumberland. Of the three north British Kingdoms of Strathclyde, centred on Dumbarton, Rheged on Solway Firth and Elmet in Leeds, only Strathclyde survived. Rheged and Elmet were overcome by the Saxon kingdom of Northumbria.

The former tribal territories of the Deceangli, Ordovices, Silures and other Celtic tribes of Wales had evolved into the kingdoms of Gwynedd, Dyfed, Powys and Gwent, all of which existed by 550. In south-western England the kingdom of Dumnonia also retained its Celtic character.

Similar kingdoms emerged in Ireland and Gaul, and all retained strong elements of their Celtic tribal affinities from pre-Roman times.

The society of western Europe in the early middle ages.

The Age of the Saints falls within the early middle ages of Britain's history, from around the third to seventh centuries, a time once known (and still known in popular usage) as 'the Dark Ages', both because of its apparently scant evidence and because this period was marked by several centuries of instability arising from the absence of uniform social, political, economic, religious or military order.

In such uncertain times, individuals and societies were amenable to any offer of possible salvation and so were open to the remedies provided by priests maintaining the pagan forms of worship as well as those of the Christian church. It was in this spiritual desolation that the Celtic Church evolved to administer Christian doctrine in a form most appropriate to the population to which it was providing pastoral care.

By the middle of the fourth century, the Roman fleet and coastal Legions had already been struggling to protect Britain's shores from invaders. There is archaeological evidence that the major Roman port of London was in decline as a consequence of raids by heavily armed sea-borne Germanic tribes. The port was originally part of the town, but as the raids increased in severity and frequency the town had to retreat behind a defensive wall, so that by around 300 AD, the port was left exposed; one may infer that it was of non strategic value.

Over the next hundred years, Roman sea power and mercantile activity in the English Channel and around the British coast virtually disappeared, leaving an undefended coast for the Saxon invaders who settled over eastern

26

England, eventually mixing with the native Celts of that area or driving out those who could not assimilate. The Roman withdrawal opened the floodgates to the invading Saxon, Angle and Jute tribes looking for land to settle. The native Romano-British and Celtic tribes also sought to fill the power vacuum left by the Roman withdrawal. The bitter fighting between the British Celtic tribes meant there was no unified resistance to the invading Saxons, who had little difficulty in defeating this weakened and disunited native force of tribal kingdoms.

The stability of the former Celtic-occupied lands of northern and western Europe, particularly Britain and northern France, was replaced by uncertainty as successive waves of invaders settled, causing native inhabitants to become even more concentrated in the more inaccessible, western parts of the country. Inaccessible, that is, by land – the long established western sea routes were still open and became even more heavily used.

Wales was also subject to invasions by pagan Irish tribes such as the Fenni, Ui Neill and Deisi, who settled along coastal areas of Wales and also penetrated inland in the southern part of the country. It was during this period that the Celtic Church had to be robust to survive in Britain and Gaul. This challenge could not have been met if the western sea routes had not remained open to the seafaring Celtic saints, thereby providing a lifeline between centres of Celtic culture and faith that would otherwise have been obliterated.

The native Brythonic population of the early middle ages held a mixture of religious beliefs which were generally Christian in the more strongly Roman influenced urban areas and pagan in the countryside. The Saxons who settled in much of eastern England were pagan and drove out the Christian factions, who sought safety by settling in the western, Celtic areas of the country, as also did many pagan British refugees.

Some of the Christian groups considered themselves to be

more Romano-Brythonic than Celtic, and so tried to maintain the Roman Church influence and continued to use Latin. Others who considered themselves to be more Brythonic than Roman reverted to the Celtic languages and customs.

In the fifth century Gaul was also under attack by pagan tribes, as Frankish invaders took hold in the north and Visigoths in the south, resulting in further groups of Christian refugees who used the western sea routes to settle in Wales, Scotland and Ireland. In the ensuing political and social upheaval the Christian faction of the re-established Celtic groups, although swelled by Romano-Brythonic and Romano-Gallo Christian factors, eventually became detached from the influence of the Christian church of Rome. This resulted in the establishment of the Brythonic Christian church and the birth of Celtic Christianity.

Early Christianity and the Celtic Church

An awareness of Christianity was widespread in the British Isles before the Roman invasion and had been introduced to Britain along the western sea routes by traders and missionaries from the Middle East or Greece. Joseph of Arimathea, one of Christ's disciples, is thought to have set up a church on the Isle of Avalon, near Glastonbury, as a base for missionary work in Britain. Joseph was a tin trader and so was likely to have travelled many times to Britain along the established trade routes. His purported journey to Avalon with twelve companions was from Palestine along one of the tin trader's routes most favoured by the Greeks, entering the Rhône at Marseilles then passing through Limoges, Provence, Aquitaine, and Brittany for the sea voyage to Cornwall.

There is a legend that, during the unrecorded period of his early life, Jesus accompanied Joseph, who was his uncle, on one of his trading visits to Britain.

It is likely that knowledge of the new Christian cult was introduced in the western area of Britain by travellers and missionaries from the Mediterranean, reaching these shores along the western sea routes. The Welsh poet Taliesin, writing around 600, stated that in 199 Christianity was known in Britain in places not accessible to the Romans, although this conflicts with the sixth-century writings of the monk Gildas, who stated that Christianity was brought to Britain by Tiberius Caesar, who died in AD 37. The foundation of a strong Christian church in Ireland, which was never colonised by the Romans, but was an established destination on the western sea routes, indicates that Taliesin may have been correct.

Christianity in Britain was first established under a Roman system based on the larger population centres, and was an organisation spreading from a central administration under the influence of Rome. As early as 313 three Brythonic Bishops attended a synod at Arles in Gaul under the authority of the Roman church.

The cult of Christianity prospered in the regions most socially Romanised. The Celtic areas of Britain were less urban, and missionaries adapted facets of the Christian faith to the population they were addressing. The former pagan practices of these areas involved both priests and priestesses, and women were therefore allowed to play a stronger part in leading the spiritual faith of their communities. The Roman Church did not admit women priests, whereas in Celtic areas there were instances of the presence of nuns before monks.

The Celtic Church, recognising the needs of its followers, developed a monastic organisation that was influenced by the traditions of St Anthony in Egypt, the first of the 'Desert Fathers'. The monastic movement reached the British Isles through missionaries such as St Martin, St Patrick and St Ninian.

The Celtic Church also accepted the practice of 'white martyrdom' which had been practiced by St Anthony in the desert and required holy men to give up all they loved – usually family, possessions and comforts – in exchange for a period of suffering and fasting. This meant seeking locations where solitude and privation would assist monks in achieving their objectives. The Celtic saints found alternative 'deserts' in the most remote or inhospitable places in order to experience the purity of existence they sought. This resulted in the establishment of many monastic cells in isolated, windy and exposed headlands or rocky offshore islands. In many Celtic areas, present-day place-names containing the word 'Dyserth' indicate this religious origin.

As well as this individual suffering and fasting to confirm that they were giving themselves to Christ, the Celtic monks were required to find converts. Schools and monasteries were formed and a network of Celtic Christian centres came into existence, which incorporated the pagan respect for nature and ecology, and developed learning, not just in religious matters but also in science, poetry and art.

The comfort and richness of the Roman church was replaced in the Celtic church by a humility and adoption of hardship as a sign of saintliness. Bishops were replaced by abbots. Cleanliness was viewed by some monks as an abhorrent, decadent state and the act of washing as an insult to their faith. Many were ridden with lice, which they regarded as 'pearls of God' and they boasted that water never touched their feet, apart from when they waded through rivers on their missionary journeys.

Eventually the Celtic Church disagreed with the Roman Church over a number of specific issues, the most important being calculation of the date of Easter.

The Roman Church did not want Easter to coincide with Passover, and so in 457 they adopted a solar rather than a lunar calendar to arrive at a different form of cyclical calculation. The Celtic Church was reluctant to follow the practice of the Roman Church and retained the original calculation, which resulted in confusion and inconvenience to Christians who wished to know that they were celebrating an important event at the correct time.

The Celtic Church did not sit comfortably with the Roman Church, as it developed incompatible ecclesiastical doctrines. Pope Celestinus sent St Germanus of Auxerre to Britain in an attempt to restore orthodox teaching. On a later occasion, when the Pope sent St Augustine to Britain on a crusade to convert pagan Saxons to Christianity, he made attempts to encourage the Celtic priests to join him in his campaign but was stoutly rebuffed. The Celtic Church would have nothing to do with either mission and became progressively more isolationist over the next 150 years.

The Celtic saints' prime purpose was to convert their fellow Celts – not the Saxons – from pagan to Christian faith, and to support and lead the spiritual well-being of the existing Christian communities. The role of the Celtic saints in leading military resistance against pagan invaders was also accepted as a fundamental activity. The Celtic Church had risen to the unique challenge presented during these early years of Christianity in Britain, and as a more unified political structure evolved its work became more effective.

Social and political allegiances

Celtic Christianity did not develop as a function of purely theological considerations; its cults were influenced by the needs of a Celtic community, and required the patronage of ruling Royal families who reflected the political geography of the time.

A Christian missionary priest could only hope to gain acceptance of his cult if he could first gain the public support of the ruling king and supplant the existing spiritual, pagan, advisor. Once the noble patronage was given – often with the granting of land for the building of a church – conversion of the general population could be tackled. This initial process was made easier when the Celtic Christian priests were themselves of noble birth, or were related by marriage to other ruling families. Many of the saints were the most educated men and women of their era, and many of the men had a military training, which allowed them to give sound advice to their noble patrons.

The work of Gildas, a monk whose Latin manuscript *De*

Excidio Britanniae (The Destruction Of Britain) was written in 540 AD, gives a fascinating account of Brythonic ruling and religious society of the era. These two aspects of post-Roman society were inexorably bound together. It would have been very difficult, perhaps even impossible, for the Christian church to make headway without the patronage of the ruling families. This did not prevent Gildas's scathingly bitter criticisms of the rulers of Brythonic kingdoms in his day, whose irresponsible behaviour he considered to have resulted in the loss of British territory to the Saxons. Two of the 'tyrants' referred to by Gildas ruled in what is now present day Wales. He described Maelgwn (Maglocunus), King of Gwynedd as 'first in evil, mightier than many in power and malice', whereas Vortipor (Vortigern or Gwrtheyrn), King of Dyfed, came in for more detailed assessment of his failures:

> Your head is already whitening as you sit upon a throne that is full of guiles and stained from top to bottom with diverse murders and adulteries, bad son of a good king Vortipor, tyrant of the Demetae. The end of your life is gradually drawing near. Why can you not be satisfied by such violent surges of sin, which you suck down like vintage wine – or rather allow yourself to be engulfed by them? Why, to crown your crimes do you weigh down your wretched soul with a burden you can not shrug off, the rape of a shameless daughter after the removal and honourable death of your own wife?

The King of Dumnonia – the early-middle-age kingdom over the present-day areas of Cornwall, Devon and Somerset – was described in a similarly disparaging way when Gildas referred to him (and even more impolitely to his mother) as 'Constantine, the tyrant whelp of the filthy Lioness of Dumnonia'.

Gildas – later acclaimed as St Gildas - clearly did not feel the need to couch his opinions in diplomatic language. In the course of his life he travelled widely through the western lands of Britain and voyaged to Ireland where he was highly respected. His manuscript could only have been written from the safety of his various retreats in south Brittany, where he spent the majority of his later years and where he was also held in high regard.

Chapter 2

CULTURAL PROVINCES

When the Romans left Britain, leaving the population to be responsible for its own administration and security, the people anticipated that they would acquire a form of 'home rule', envisaging that theirs would be a unified country of Britons, possibly retaining some Roman customs but essentially returning to their Celtic heritage in those regions which had not been completely Romanised. This was demonstrated by the civil war which broke out in the kingdom of Strathclyde when the Christian king, Rhydderch Hael, was challenged by two pagan princes who believed they represented the 'true Britons'. However, the people of Britain were to be bitterly disappointed and their despair, referred to earlier, must have been overwhelming. Instead of unity, the country was fragmented and weakened by continuous, bloody warfare between the Brythonic kingdoms. Whilst the Brythons were engaged in slaughtering each other, the Picts took the opportunity to expand into southern Scotland and northern England, Saxons arrived on the east and south coasts, and Irish tribes invaded the west. It was not long before the Brythons found themselves in a worse state then they had ever been as a Roman colony; they lost more and more territory to the Germanic tribes in particular. The surviving Brythonic kingdoms became concentrated in the western and northern parts of the country, and the cultural provinces which then evolved played a distinctive role in shaping the development of Christianity in the British Isles.

The concept of cultural areas or provinces has been

developed by a number of illustrious geographers, social anthropologists and historians, such as A. Downes, Sir Cyril Fox and E. G. Bowen, and the latter has identified, in the Age of the Saints, a number of major cultural areas which are allied to the western sea routes.

These distinct cultural provinces retained the remnants of the Celtic society once enjoyed by the Irish, Brythons and Gauls, and facilitated by use of the western sea routes. The Celtic saints were active in these provinces and sub-provinces, which overlapped regions that in modern-day terms can be described as Wales, Ireland, northern Britain, Brittany and a northwest Europe province.

The area now within the boundary of modern-day Wales was, in the post-Roman period, a group of Brythonic kingdoms of Celtic origin which, during Roman times, had evolved from the former tribal areas such as those of the Silures and Ordovices. The northern part of Wales was ruled by the powerful kingdoms of Gwynedd, Powys and Ceredigion, whilst the dominant kingdoms of mid and south Wales were Dyfed, Brycheiniog, Glywysing, Gwent and Erging. In the south-western of England the kingdom of Dumnonia had developed from the Celtic tribal area of the same name.

These kingdoms would ultimately be the only Celtic/Brythonic kingdoms in the south of the country to maintain an effective resistance against the Germanic tribes, who, as they conquered and settled, consolidated their hold by establishing Saxon kingdoms such as Mercia, Northumbria and Wessex. In the north of Britain the Brythons kingdoms of Strathclyde, Rheged and Gododdin, all deriving from a predominantly Celtic population, also maintained fierce resistance to the Saxon onslaught but were eventually overwhelmed.

The Border between the Brythons and the Saxons

The eastern borders with Saxon lands had to be fiercely defended because the success of the Saxon army at the Battle

TRIBAL KINGDOMS - circa 600

of Dyrham, near Bristol in 577 resulted in the burning of the Brythonic-held towns of Bath and Gloucester and the loss of all land east of the river Severn, apart from Dumnonia which was now cut off from fellow Brythons in Wales and the north. The Saxons and Angles now occupied land up to the eastern shore of the Severn. They were determined to drive their way across to the Irish Sea, but in the south their progress was blocked by Prince Iddon of Gwent, assisted by St Teilo.

In the north of the country the Saxon quest to fight their way to the Irish Sea succeeded at the Battle of Chester, when Powys was defeated and the monks of Bangor Is-coed were massacred. Wales was also now isolated from the Old North, and at this point the western sea routes became the only means of contact between these western areas of former Celtic Britain.

In southern Wales these unsettled times were made worse by numerous invasions of the far west by pagan Irish tribes such as the Deisi. These tribes were not raiders, but prospective settlers, who sometimes emphasized this by the practice of 'burning their boats' on the beaches where they landed.

The old Roman town and military base of Caerleon in south-eastern Wales retained a Christian settlement, which had been well established at an early date; however, this centre of Christianity was close to the border with the Saxon lands just to the east of the river Wye. Christian communities of south Wales also wished to maintain contact with the remnants of Celtic Brythonic communities concentrated now in Dumnonia (Cornwall), but contact by land was difficult and dangerous, for the east bank of the Severn estuary was under Saxon occupation.

Sea transport from southern Wales to Cornwall was therefore the only option available. As well as the desire to maintain contact with Celtic communities in Cornwall, there was also the essential requirement of retaining friendly ports of refuge and embarkation ports for the frequent voyages to Gaul.

The difficulty became even more pronounced after the seventh century, when the territory held by the Saxons spread further westwards along the southern shore of the Bristol Channel into areas previously held by the Brythons, who were forced to retreat even further down into the south west peninsula. Ports and landings in the upper reaches of the Channel were therefore increasingly taken and held by Saxons, and the Celtic monks and abbots were denied a crossing from south Wales. As a result, the seafaring monks had to sail further westwards before being able to make a safe landfall on the north Cornish coast. The exposed passage from Wales to Cornwall therefore became longer, and consequently more dangerous.

Wales Northern Province
(Gwynedd, Powys, Dyfed
and the 'Old North' – Yr Hen Ogledd)

The people of northern Wales had more cultural and political affinity with those of northern England and southern Scotland (the Old North – Yr Hen Ogledd), from whom they were now cut off by land, than they did with their countrymen in southern Wales.

From around 400 to 450 the north Brythonic chieftain, Cunedda of the Votadini tribe (the Gododdin), moved from Manaw Gododdin, now Clackmannanshire, in central Scotland, with eight of his nine sons and his army of warriors and cavalry, to take control of the whole of northern Wales, where his family was to form the basis of what would become a royal court. It is likely that Cunedda's Votadini were already Christians as a result of the Romano-Gallo missionary work of Ninian in the fourth century, and the tribe may also have been incorporated into the Roman Legionary structure as 'Foederati' under Magnus Maximus in the days of Cunedda's grandfather. Cunedda's military campaign and settlement in northern Wales appears to have been in response to a Roman request to secure the area against Irish invaders, particularly the Scotti tribe, because troops had been withdrawn from the Legionary base at Segontium (Caernarfon). The names of both Cunedda and Magnus Maximus appear prominently in the story of Christianity in Wales, and their families not only provided patronage of Christian saints, but many of their descendants also became saints.

The patronage of Christian saints by royal families is shown by the actions of Maelgwn Gwynedd, the sixth-century prince of the House of Cunedda, who gave the old Roman fort on Holy Island, Anglesey, to St Cybi to build his church. He also allowed a Christian church to be built at the site of the Roman fort of Caerhun in the Conwy valley, granted land to Kentigern to build a monastery at St Asaph, and gave land for a monastery at Rhos-on-Sea (Llandrillo-yn-Rhos).

Old Roman sites were often favoured for establishing Christian churches, probably because they were on good communication routes, and were generally near centres of population. Perhaps they were also still imbued with a sense of order and power. This practice was also seen in the south of Wales at Caerleon and Caerwent in Gwent.

The cultural links between northern Wales and the 'Old North' were unbroken, and became strengthened by further population movements from the 'Old North' as a response to the increasing success of Pict and Saxon campaigns. Another north British king to settle in northern Wales was Pabo Post Prydain (the Pillar of the Britons) who was driven from his kingdom by invading Picts and sought refuge in northern Wales where he became a monk. He died as St Pabo in 595 and his church of Llanbabo is one of the oldest dedications on Anglesey.

Men of Gwynedd are also believed to have joined the army of the Gododdin in their ill-fated attempt to displace the Saxons from their stronghold at Catraeth. The Welsh poet Aneirin, who wrote of the heroic but disastrous defeat of the Gododdin tribe at that battle, became part of the refugee movement from southern Scotland to northern Wales.

Although pagan beliefs had been supplanted by Roman

Christianity, they were not entirely vanquished. Consequently, when the Roman Legions were withdrawn, pagan practice became increasingly resurgent and was re-established in many areas. Some prominent men of influential families re-adopted paganism. This led to civil war in the Kingdom of Strathclyde, where the pagan prince Gwenddoleu raised an army, which he and his followers claimed represented true Brythons (the pre-Roman Celtic inhabitants of the area), to challenge the Christian king, Rhydderch Hael. The pagan force alleged that Rhydderch was not an even-handed ruler but favoured Christians, particularly the Romano-Britons who were descended from the Roman colonists, and the former Legionaries drafted into the area to defend Hadrian's Wall who had remained in the area when the Roman troops were withdrawn. The two sides were therefore divided on both ethnic and religious lines, with Rhydderch Hael standing for Romano-Brythonic Christian interests and Gwenddoleu the upholder of Brythonic pagan beliefs. The two armies met at the battle of Arderydd around 575 on the west bank of the Esk to the north of Carlisle.

Rhydderch Hael was victorious and as his stature grew – following further victories protecting his land and his subjects – he became the highly respected King of the Old North (Brenin Yr Hen Ogledd). In the aftermath of the battle of Arderydd, St Kentigern, who had previously left the kingdom for north Wales in order to escape the pagan uprising, was summoned by Rhydderch Hael back to Strathclyde to help him banish paganism and re-establish Christianity throughout the kingdom.

On his death, Rhydderch Hael was laid to rest on consecrated ground in Llŷn, northern Wales, alongside the western sea routes. Local legend tells that a Neolithic burial chamber close to Y Ffôr near Pwllheli was also used as the burial chamber for Rhydderch Hael and this is referred to in 'Canu Llywarch Hen', a collection of Welsh poetry from the ninth century. An alternative story tells of Rhydderch Hael being buried at one of the oldest churches in the area, Abererch, which also has other royal associations and is dedicated to Sant Cawrdaf, Tywysog Brycheiniog (Prince of Brecon). As recently as the nineteenth century Manx fishermen landing at the port of Pwllheli would pay homage at the church of Abererch to Rhydderch Hael, who was regarded as a saviour of the Isle of Man after he defeated a Northumbrian king.

The Llŷn area of northern Wales also had an Irish association – its name is derived from Leinster – and there are remains of Iron Age round huts from around 600 BC known as 'Cytiau Gwyddelod' (Huts of the Irish), although there are no Irish archaeological finds. Nevertheless settlement here by Irish people is in accord with the folk heritage of this area of northern Wales. There are many Iron Age hill forts in Llŷn, and Tre'r Ceiri was one of the chief Iron Age fortifications in Europe. Llŷn is also associated with the sons of Cunedda. It is therefore most likely to have experienced a history of invasion of Irish tribes who were then expelled by the house of Cunedda during the post-Roman period.

The background of St Tysilio, son of King Brochfael of Powys, one of the most powerful northern kingdoms of the sixth century, gives an insight into the turbulence of the times in which the saints lived. Although the Powys family was almost certainly Christian, this did not prevent Brochfael from waging constant cruel and bloody wars against his neighbours. In sixth-century Britain, fighting was a way of life for the royal families. In the east they fought against Saxon invaders and in the west against Irish raiders. Most often, and unfortunately for the Celtic Brythons, they fought each other.

Whilst Tysilio was engaged in his religious work, his brother, Cynan, who succeeded their father, Brochfael, as King of Powys, was leading an entirely different way of life – wreaking violent and bloody havoc amongst neighbouring kingdoms. As discussed later, this eventually had dire consequences for Christian life in northern Wales, and a dramatic effect on Tysilio's own future.

The poet Taliesin records that the armies of Tysilio's brother, Cynan, had waged war against the kingdoms of Gwent, Anglesey, Dyfed, Cornwall and Brycheiniog, whose men were defeated and slaughtered in battle. These wars were conducted against Cynan's fellow Brythons amongst whom the Kingdom of Powys had become feared and hated. The legacy of these wars was passed on to Cynan's son, Selyf (Tysilio's nephew), who was placed in the unfortunate position of having to defend Powys against Aethelfrith, the Saxon king of Northumbria, whose expansionist forays into the west were as ferocious and determined as those conducted by Selyf's father against his neighbours. Aethelfrith wanted to create a Kingdom of Northumbria which would stretch from coast to coast. As he marched into the west, he pushed the Brythons before him until it became clear that a desperate last stand had to be made by the Kingdom of Powys at Chester on the river Dee.

By this time, the battles waged by Powys had seriously weakened the ability of the Brythons of the area to resist Saxon attack and, in any event, such was the animosity caused by Cynan's previous actions against his neighbours that none of the native kings or princes would now go to the aid of his son Selyf, who had no choice but to meet the army of Aethelfrith without support. However, Selyf's army was not entirely alone, because monks from the monastery of Bangor Is-coed, lying within the Kingdom of Powys some twenty miles upstream of Chester, attended the battlefield to issue their prayers in support of the men of Powys.

Aethelfrith was probably more worried by the monks' prayers than by Selyf's warriors, and he therefore attacked the unarmed and undefended monks first, slaughtering them where they stood, before turning his attention to the army of Powys. Aethelfrith's force was too strong for the defenders and the King of Powys was defeated and killed at Chester in around 616. The victorious Aethelfrith, a pagan, set about a campaign of brutal subjection and ordered the slaughter of all of the remaining monks at Bangor Is-Coed. An account by Bede suggests that up to one thousand two hundred monks were put to the sword (other accounts put the number of monks killed at two hundred and the date of the battle of Chester at 607, with Powys supported by the kings of Dumnonia, Dyfed and Gwynedd).

Aethelfrith's successor, Edwin, continued the westwards campaign, eventually invading Anglesey and laying siege to Cadwallon, son of Cadfan, on Ynys Seiriol (Puffin Island) in 629. Cadwallon held out and was later able to expel Edwin from Anglesey. After joining forces with the pagan King Penda of Mercia, Cadwallon pursued Edwin and went on to kill him at the battle of Meigen, near Doncaster in 632. Cadwallon also killed Edwin's successors, Osric and Eanfrith in 633, and declared his aim of exterminating all the Saxon invaders in Britain. However, in 634 Cadwallon was killed by Eanfrith's brother, Oswald, and although succeeded by his son, Cadwaladr, these events appear to have marked a turning point against the Brythons, for the Kingdom of Powys had by then been brought to its lowest ebb.

The human suffering during this period was immense, and it was a time of great uncertainty and sorrow for the population at all levels of society. The Welsh poems of Princess Heledd of Powys recounting the destruction of the Royal Court at Pengwern by Saxons, and the death of her brother Prince Cynddylan in the service of King Penda, speak volumes about the despair and anguish felt by all Brythons at that time:

'My brothers were slain at one stroke,
Cynan, Cynddylan, Cynwraith,
Defending Tren, ravaged town

More common was blood on the field's face
Than ploughing of fallow
The hall of Cynddylan, dark is the roof,

Since the Saxon cut down
Powys's Cynddylan and Elfan....'

Within the Wales/Northern cultural province there were a number of monastic centres that developed into mother churches at concentrations of large populations, such as St Asaph, Caergybi, Penmon, Bangor, Clynnog, Tywyn, Llanbadarn Fawr and Whithorn. There were also a number of well known cults associated with voyaging saints such as Seiriol, Cadfan, Tysilio, Deiniol, Kentigern and Ninian, and cults of apparently exclusively land-based saints such as Beuno, who was more of a walker than a voyager, and led large groups of followers on foot.

The cultural affinities were founded on the ease of movement along the western sea routes, particularly those passing across the Irish Sea, which is bounded by the coasts of northern Wales and Cardigan Bay, the western areas of Cumbria and southern Scotland and the east coast of Ireland. As well as providing the seaways for the travellers between the Old North and Wales, the Irish Sea also carried Irish tribes who settled in Scotland and Wales. The formation of the Kingdom of Dalriada in western Scotland by the Irish (Scotti) eventually brought a unified influence to the country, while settlements in southwest Wales by the Deisi were effective in founding the kingdom of Dyfed. The Irish Fenni invaded and settled in northern Wales but this did not result in any permanent effect on the cultural life of the region, for it is clear that one of the prime reasons for the later arrival of Cunedda and his men was to drive out the Irish settlers. The fact that there are now only a few linguistic indications of the previous Irish presence there suggests that this was a successful strategy.

The Southern Wales Cutural Province
(Gwent, Erging, Glywysing, Brycheiniog, Dyfed and Dumnonia)

Whereas northern Wales in the early middle ages looked

culturally and politically to the Old North, the kingdoms of Gwent, Erging and Glywysing of southern Wales had their affinities with Leinster and Munster of southern and eastern Ireland and the kingdom of Dumnonia on the south-western peninsula of England. Even within southern Wales there were discernable differences between the south-eastern kingdoms of Gwent, Erging and Glywysing lying in the more Romanised areas, and the kingdoms of Brycheiniog and Dyfed in central and western Wales, where Irish and Romano-Gallic influences were more prevalent.

The harbours, inlets and beaches of southern Wales do not lie on the Irish Sea but look out across what was, in the early middle ages, called the Northern Sea (now the Bristol Channel) to the northern coastlines of Somerset, Devon and Cornwall. The Bristol Channel narrows to the east as it merges into the estuary of the river Severn, and to the west opens out into the St George's Channel and the approaches from the Atlantic. The old name of 'Northern Sea' for the Bristol Channel reflected the geographical prominence of the south-western peninsula of Devon and Cornwall, which reached out to the Atlantic, and filled mariners with trepidation if they were called upon to voyage around its most westerly points of Lands End and Cape Cornwall. It was such a significant land mass that it was seen to separate the 'Southern Sea', also known as the 'Sea of Ichtus' lying to the south of the peninsula, from the 'Northern Sea', which was the Bristol Channel and Irish Sea to the north.

As in the north of the country, the south also had ancient cultural links with other regions along the western sea routes as is indicated by the succession of Neolithic cromlechs and standing stones, and Bronze and Iron Age hill forts. Distinctive Late Bronze Age socketed axes ornamented with three converging ribs (1,000-500 BC) were manufactured in south-eastern Wales and have been found in Cornwall, the Dee Valley, East Anglia and the Channel Islands. The design of the later hill forts indicate that the Veneti tribe of southern Brittany were influencing or controlling significant areas of the land adjoining the Severn estuary, and as they were the foremost maritime and trading Celtic tribe, their extension into southern Britain would have been a natural development.

The south-eastern coastal areas of Gwent and Glywysing (present-day south Glamorgan) were the only parts of Wales where the Roman occupation was not solely military, but also civic. There were large urban towns at Caerwent and Caerleon and numerous villas, indicating a settled and stable society. Christianity was organized on Roman principles, and this continued after the withdrawal of the Legions. Rather than return to Celtic ways, the area became even more Romanised with the arrival of refugees from east of the Severn who were fleeing from advancing Saxon forces.

Physical geography influenced the cultural links of the people of southern Wales, who were remote both by sea and by land from the Old North and the north of Ireland, but over thousands of years had established trade and cultural links with south and southwest England and beyond. Close to the site of Illtud's monastery at Llanilltud Fawr is Dinas Powys, which at the time was the seat of the King of Glywysing, where archaeological remains have been found originating from Alexandria, Athens and Bordeaux. This area of south-eastern Wales had been entirely Romanised up to the departure of the Legions, and it clearly retained its cosmopolitan outlook, including trade of goods and ideas, after they left.

While the Roman colonisation of Britain may have resulted in the dilution of Celtic culture in south-eastern Wales and southern England generally, it did not place any bar on the continuation of trade and social exchanges. The subsequent invasion and settlement of Saxon people in southern England, particularly around the north Somerset and Avon regions, had a far more significant effect as they took control over land routes previously used by the Celtic Brythons. British refugees who were being forced westwards made their way into Gwent, Erging and Glywysing, just as

ROMAN WALES

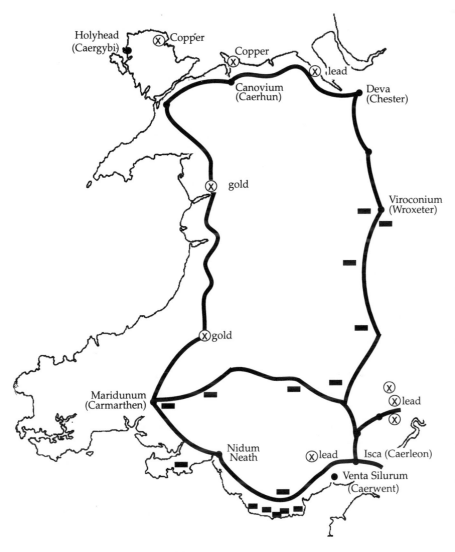

Holyhead (Caergybi) — Ⓧ Copper

Copper Ⓧ

Ⓧ lead

Canovium (Caerhun)

Deva (Chester)

Ⓧ gold

Viroconium (Wroxeter)

Ⓧ gold

Maridunum (Carmarthen)

Ⓧ
Ⓧ lead
Ⓧ

Nidum Neath

Ⓧ lead

Isca (Caerleon)

Venta Silurum (Caerwent)

Ⓧ - copper, lead & gold mines

▬ - villas

〜 - major roads

those in the north sought refuge in Gwynedd and Powys.

Fortunately the resurgence in use of the western sea routes at this time maintained the cultural and religious affinities between southern Wales and south-western England, where Brythonic customs were becoming increasingly concentrated into the kingdom of Dumnonia. The sea routes across the Bristol Channel and St George's Channel to Ireland from Cornwall and south-western Wales remained unaffected.

Wales in the early middle-ages clearly had distinct cultural differences and affinities between north and south, with the south being further sub-divided between east and west. The north of the country reached out to embrace its fellow Brythons in southern Scotland and northern Ireland, whilst the south maintained its links with southern Ireland and Cornwall. All areas were of course interlinked with each other and with other areas such as Armorica (Brittany), and all were bound with the common aim of installing or maintaining Christianity amongst the former Celtic and Brythonic populations.

However, distinctive regional cults did develop and were reflected in various elements in the emerging Celtic Church. The southern Wales cults that were developed by the saints known as the Children of Brychan – the Dyfrig/ Cadog/ Illtud tradition and the Dewi(David)/Teilo tradition – did not make any progress in northern Wales. The cults of Teilo and Dewi were particularly strong in south-western Wales but were unable to make any impact in north Wales – for example Dewi had no dedications north of the river Wyre, which seems to have been a political boundary beyond which he did not cross. A different cultural province had evolved there under the influence of leaders from the Old North, such as Rhydderch Hael and Cunedda. The patronage of successive generations of Cunedda's family was offered to the favoured northern Brythonic saints, although the Dewi/Teilo cult was later linked to the House of Cunedda by family marriages.

There may also have been language barriers between north and south, with different dialects of Celtic speech, and indeed that would have been a problem to be overcome by the southern Wales cults of Dewi, Cadog and Illtud, living alongside Goedelic settlers and the followers of the Irish 'Children of Brychan.' They would have worked to achieve converts not just to Christianity but perhaps also to Brythonic speech.

Most saints were Brythonic-speaking, but the Irish were Goedelic, and this form of Celtic language may have been introduced into south-western Wales by the large movements of the Irish tribes who settled there, particularly during the time when Ogham was being inscribed on stones. Irish Christians had visited south-western Wales in Roman and post-Roman times. There was a strong Irish tradition of travel along the Roman road following the river Teifi to reach the Brecon area where the Irish-influenced Kingdom of Brychan was founded. The Irish influence may have also penetrated the coastal plain of southern Wales, for there are Goedelic traces of speech and custom in southeast Wales. It is the Irish form of Illtud's name which is preserved in 'Llanyltwyt' or 'Llanitwyt', before it was reduced to the present-day Llantwit Major.

St Brynach was an Irish nobleman who converted to Christianity then settled in south-western Wales where, at his church in Nevern, there are two stones inscribed in both Ogham and Latin. There are also church dedications to Brynach in Dyfed, Powys and South Glamorgan where he is referred to as Brynach Wyddel (Brynach the Irishman).

The Life of St Cadog – The Vita Sancti Cadoci – also tells of Cadog's frequent trips to Ireland and the Irish saints Finnian of Clonard and Cainnech (associated with Patrick) were disciples at Cadog's Llancarfan.

Gaulish Immigrants

The Kingdom of Dyfed to the west had many natural harbours lying on St George's Channel and the western

Atlantic approaches, and received an influx of Christian missionaries and refugees from two quite distinct geographical areas – Gaul and Ireland.

Just as the collapse of the western part of the Roman Empire had left Britain exposed to pagan Saxon invaders, the Christian regions of Gaul were being overrun by Frankish invaders who were also pagan; Christian refugees were forced to use the western sea routes to escape to western Britain where safety was still to be found. These immigrants from Gaul brought with them a combination of Romano-Gallic practices, as well as some cult followers of the ascetic monastic movement which had experienced antagonism from traditional Christian sects. However, both sects were metaphorically – perhaps literally – now in the same boat.

These international links were maintained by sea, from small ports, such as Porth-clais, which served the Christian centre of Menevia (St Davids); Tenby, which was a terminus on one of the trans-peninsula routes, and the sheltered ports of Milford Haven, such as Dale, which are still in use today. Maridunum (Carmarthen) would have been an international trading port. There was also a transit route over the peninsula from the mouth of the Taf in Carmarthenshire to the Gwaun estuary of Pembrokeshire. It was an area attractive to Celtic Saints – not only those seeking large communities to convert or serve, but also those seeking their 'desert retreat', such as St Govan, whose chapel on the cliff-side near Milford Haven was a small, dark cell where isolation and contemplation were possible.

Irish Immigrants

As immigrants were arriving from continental Europe, other groups were voyaging along the seaways from the west, making the short passage from south-eastern Ireland to south-western Wales. The monk Nennius had recorded that this area had already been settled by the Irish pagan tribes of the Deisi and the Ui Neill for centuries, but they and the remainder of the native population were now receiving the attention of Irish Christian missionaries approaching Britain with an energetic zeal.

The missionaries adopted a clear plan when seeking converts from pagan populations: win over the chieftain, depose the pagan priest, and erect a church, preferably on land granted by the ruling family so that it was seen to have authority.

Having landed on the western coast of Wales, these two groups of Christians – the Romano-Gallic and the Irish – used the old Roman roads to make progress into south Wales, motivated either by the search for converts or for land to settle. The richest agricultural land of the Vale of Glamorgan and Gwent was already occupied and these Romano-Gallic and Irish immigrants were not of a warlike disposition, so tended to move inland, creating new communities.

The Romano-Gallic and Irish missionaries, having landed at one of the western Wales havens such as Porth-clais would make their way to the old Roman town of Maridunum (Carmarthen) and follow the Roman road eastwards, up the Tywi valley to Llandovery where they would trek over the watershed to reach the headwaters of the river Usk and follow its southeasterly course to Abergavenny and Monmouth. There was also a southerly route along the coast from Maridunum to Loughor and on to the former Roman towns of Caerleon and Caerwent where, in the Roman colonial days, a ferry at Aust crossed the Severn to the Bristol area and the security of the Roman fort at Portishead. During Roman times travellers could continue eastwards to Bath, Marlborough, Silchester, London, Canterbury and the channel port of Richborough, where a crossing to Gaul could be made.

The fact that this route was at some time used by Irish travellers and settlers to south central England is indicated by the find of an Ogham-inscribed stone in a well at Silchester. This was inscribed in a similar style to the Ogham stones in Breconshire, southeast Wales. The Irish moving eastwards met the westward-bound refugees from Gloucestershire, Cirencester and Bath, which led to an eclectic mixture of cult ideas.

A major reason for the original construction of these routes by the Romans was to facilitate the export of the large amounts of gold mined at Dolaucothi in west Wales to Rome, but even after the withdrawal of the Legions the roads were still major arteries of communication for the British Kingdoms.

The Ireland Cultural Province

Since prehistoric times Ireland was a major destination on the western sea routes and, like Britain, Gaul and Galicia, it went through the same stages of cultural development to become a Celtic country, sharing common heritage and trading links. There are, however, two major distinguishing features in this cultural development, because Ireland was never conquered or occupied by the Roman Empire, nor did it receive the full extent of Germanic pagan invasions suffered by Britain and Gaul in the post-Roman period. Consequently Ireland's Celtic traditions were not diluted by colonisation, Roman administration or Saxon-Germanic pagan influx, and it remained a predominantly rural society, maintaining its Celtic tribal structure.

As in other Celtic lands, the druids had been the spiritual leaders and advisors to kings. The Celtic priests sought to adopt this role, and so needed to win the support of the ruling chieftains, and adapt some practices to reflect the particular kind of early Christianity which could be compelling to a previously pagan population. One example is that of the role of the druids in cursing enemies of the king. In this respect the Irish monk St Findchua became acknowledged as one of the most famous 'Battle priests'. Legend tells that when Findchua cursed the enemy army facing his patron, the King of Meath, 'sparks of fire burst forth from his teeth, slaying their warriors, burning their ships and making a cairn of their heads.'

Findchua was subsequently recruited by the King of Leinster to curse for him in his battles, which proved successful. As his reputation grew he cursed on behalf of the King of Munster in his battle with the King of Ulster. St Findchua rode into battle in a chariot, with curses streaming from his lips. He was afterwards known as 'The Slaughterous Hero.' Similarly, St Aidan was the official curser of Brandubh, the Christian King of Leinster, at the Battle of Dunboig in 598.

On other occasions, priests were called upon to assist in what conventional Christianity of today might view as un-Christian objectives, such as the time when, due to a famine caused by a growing population and failed crops, three Kings instructed St Fechin to speak to God. The prayer was: 'to reduce the numbers of the lower class so the rest would live more comfortably.'

St Fechin obliged, but in the plague of 637 that followed the nobility were more afflicted than 'the lower class', with the result that the three kings and the saint himself were all infected and died.

Christianity developed in Ireland at about the same time as in the other, Roman-occupied, parts of the British Isles, and so was incorporated into a Celtic way of life which otherwise remained largely unchanged. The blend of Christian worship which developed there was as appropriate to Ireland as it was to the Celtic areas of Western Europe that had been incorporated into the Roman Empire. The inference is that Ireland was not isolated by its independent position outside Roman administration, nor did it lose any of its affinity or contact with other Celtic areas. The development of early Christianity was universal, reflecting the communication of philosophical and intellectual change along an independent channel – the western seaways.

The two sea routes by which Christianity reached Ireland are quite distinct: the shortest and most well-used being across the Irish Sea from southern Scotland, Wales or

Cornwall to the south-eastern coast areas of Arklow, Ardglas and Dublin, while the longer was the Atlantic route from Gaul or the Mediterranean to the Irish south coast, but it is not possible to determine which route was dominant. The most significant feature of the voyaging of Irish saints is not the manner in which Christianity was taken to Ireland, but how it evolved *within* Ireland, and was then taken to Britain and continental Europe by successions of energetic, highly motivated Irish monks.

There are not as many geographical sources of information for the tracing of the Christian development of Ireland as there are in Wales, Scotland or Brittany. While in Ireland there are a number of specific religious designations such as 'Domnach', 'Tempeall', 'Diseart' or 'Disert' – 'Church of the Desert' – which might identify an origin of Christian worship, these do not assist in identifying an individual saint. Nor are there the same frequencies of Christian place-name or locality references or references to specific saints as there are in Wales, Cornwall and Brittany: historians and geographers attempting to reconstruct the activities of Irish saints in Ireland do not have the wealth of clues indicated by the widespread tradition of Welsh 'Llans', Breton 'Kers' and Scottish 'Cils'. In contrast, the majority of Irish churches are named after topographical features rather than dedications to saints. The naming of Irish churches generally reflects geographical association, such as 'Church of Miloc', where 'Miloc' is not a saint but derives from the old Irish term for a low-lying marshy area of land or being adjacent to a river – hence 'Church by the River'. Fortunately the Irish monasteries produced a wealth of Irish Christian literature which provides other evidence.

In Ireland two distinct philosophical provinces emerged, with the north of the country strongly influenced by the Roman church teachings of Patrick and Palladius, and the south influenced by the monastic ideals introduced directly from Gaul or the Middle East or by the saints of southern Wales. In central Ireland there was a fusion of the Roman ideas of the north and the monastic traditions of the south incorporated by St Finnian of Clonard, who combined the rigid discipline that the Celtic Church had adopted from eastern asceticism with the classical learning of the Roman tradition. Finnian's monastery at Clonard was well-placed to receive travellers from all over Ireland and from overseas, for the harbours of County Meath were well established on the western sea routes. The acclaim of Finnian's monastery as a centre of learning equalled that of Illtud's in Wales. The 'Lives of the Saints', in *The Book of Lismore* records that:

> The saints of Ireland came to Finnian from every point to learn wisdom, so that there were three thousand along with him and from them he chose twelve high bishops of Ireland. And the learned and the writings declare that no one of those three thousand went from him without a crosier, or a gospel, or some well-known sign and around those reliquaries they built their churches and their monasteries afterwards.

The monastic ideas that developed in the deserts of the eastern Mediterranean and that were introduced to western Europe through Spain took a strong hold in Gaul in the fourth century. A number of influences such as barbarian invasion and antagonism from existing Roman Church ideas resulted in refugees and missionaries from Gaul taking their monastic ideas into southern Ireland. This form of Christian worship was enthusiastically taken up in rural areas with a strong Celtic tribal culture, particularly so in Ireland where there had been no strong Roman tradition. Anchorites were associated with the larger monasteries which developed as monastic ideas spread.

The development of self-sustaining monastic communities reflecting the cult of a particular founder saint was far more appropriate to the Irish rural culture than the Roman system of bishops based in towns and presiding over largely urban dioceses, a system that existed over much of western Europe.

Despite the emergence of the monastic ideals, linguistic evidence suggests that it is likely that Christianity first reached Ireland in the south and the east by missionaries of the Roman Christian traditions. A number of churches around Dublin were founded by missionaries from Wales, who had taken the shortest crossings of the Irish Sea, and in the southern parts of the country there was a greater influence from Gaul.

Germanus of Auxerre, during one of his visits to Britain, where he had an evangelical interest in nurturing Roman Christianity, learned of the early roots of Christianity developing in Ireland. St Patrick had taken the Roman philosophy to Armagh in northeast Ireland in 432. Germanus reported back to Pope Celestinus with a recommendation that assistance should be given to the newly emerging church there. Celestinus agreed and, probably on the advice of Germanus, dispatched Palladius, a bishop of his own church in Auxerre, Gaul.

It is significant that Palladius was sent to work with those who were 'already believing in Christ', and so was clearly not required to seek new converts but to consolidate the existing belief. His was clearly not the first Roman influence in Ireland, because Latin words such as 'crimther' (priest) and 'Cresen' (Christian) were in use in the Irish language before his visit, although there was no word for 'bishop' before the arrival of Palladius. Palladius founded three churches in Ireland – one is known as a domhnach, one a ceall and the third a Teach Romhanach – and these different names demonstrate the fusion of Romano-Celtic Christian cultures within Ireland. The word domhnach, deriving from the Latin dominicum or church, is of Roman origin (and was also in use before the visit of Palladius) whilst the ceall – from which the place-name prefix 'Kil' is derived – has the Celtic meaning of 'monastic cell'. The Teach Romhanach translates from the Irish language as 'Roman House'. Palladius voyaged to Ireland from Auxerre, landing in the vicinity of Arklow – the Wicklow ports were closest to western Britain – and evangelised the Midlands and Leinster.

Three other Gaulish bishops voyaged to Ireland at about the same time as Palladius, and all went via south Wales. They were Secundinus, who established a church at Dunehaughlin (Domhnach Sechnaill – Church of Sechnaill), County Meath; Auxilius, who founded a church at Killashee in Kildare, and Isernius, who is associated with Clonmore in County Carlow.

Palladius and the other three bishops followed the Pembroke to Wicklow route.

St Isernius is commemorated at St Issels near Tenby in south-western Wales, a port on the trans-peninsula route of Pembrokeshire, and Auxilius has a dedication at Llanhernin in the parish of Llanegad (which is the oldest dedication in Wales) lying in the Tywi valley.

In many areas of Ireland, just as on the British mainland, the old druidic ways re-surfaced and there was a reversion to paganism, which so concerned the Irish High King Ainmire that he appealed to the Welsh monk Gildas for assistance in stemming the decline. Gildas, who was revered in Ireland and had supervised many of the Welsh-trained Irish saints, responded by sending many monks from the south Wales monasteries of Llancarfan and Menevia to bolster Christian practices in Ireland.

This route from south-western Wales to Ireland was also used by Welsh saints carrying monastic ideals, such as Cadog and David, and the saints known collectively as the Children of Brychan, who reached the southern Wales ports along the Tywi valley route-way from Brecon and founded many churches dedicated to Brychan.

The Brittany Gaul Cultural Province

Two bishops of Gaul, Martin of Tours and his disciple Ninian, had a significant impact on the establishment of the early Celtic Church in Britain and Ireland. Ninian, who was a native Romano-Briton and had undertaken a pilgrimage to

Rome as a young man, was trained by Martin and sent to Galloway in 398 to found a church at Whithorn. Ninian's cult assisted in the foundation of the Christian faith in the north of Britain.

St Patrick followed Ninian, carrying out his missionary work in Ireland after receiving training in France, as had Palladius, who was sent to Ireland by Pope Celestinus in 431. As Celestinus had also sent Germanus of Auxerre to Britain just two years previously, it can be seen that the interaction between the two countries does not appear to have been affected by the geographical barrier which the English Channel and Atlantic approaches presented.

In the fifth century, Cadfan, a Breton abbot, migrated from Brittany to Wales with a group of disciples. Cadfan landed at Tywyn on Cardigan Bay – the beaches, river estuaries and ports of this area being regular landing stages for shipping following the western sea routes. Cadfan's church was founded here. He and his disciples also established a large monastery on Bardsey Island (Ynys Enlli), at the northern extremity of Cardigan Bay.

As Christianity flourished in Wales and Ireland and the famous teaching monasteries such as Llanilltud Fawr in Wales and Clonmacnois in Ireland became established, the axis of Celtic Christianity moved from Gaul to Britain.

These religious connections were founded on long-standing social and political ties, because in many ways Brittany and Normandy were virtually a cultural extension of Britain. Royal families were closely related, and it was not uncommon for the younger sons of kings and princes of Britain to move to northern Gaul to acquire land and estates. Brittany was colonised by Brythons in the fifth and sixth centuries, and there were large population movements from around 450 onwards. In some cases the stimulus came from two plagues which had swept through Britain, but there was also the increasing competition for good agricultural land following invasions by north Germanic, Pictish and Irish tribes. Some population movements were by individual wealthy families and their households, but there were also large-scale movements, such as that of the Cornovii tribe from south-eastern Wales to the Vannes area of Brittany. The Cornovii were Christians and there were many dedications to members of St Gildas's family in their homeland. They were Romanised and had supplied the manpower to form the Chors I Cornoviorum Legion which defended Hadrian's Wall. They occupied the districts of Wales – the south-eastern borderlands – that were most under attack from Saxons, and their leaders decided to leave and colonise a new area rather than face incessant warfare in Britain.

The British immigrants settled in forest clearings, and their leaders were accompanied by saints who negotiated settlement rights with the existing rulers of local tribes. Most of Armorica was Roman Christian and the Celtic Christians settled alongside them after landing on Brittany's peninsulas, rias and islands.

The founding saints of north Brittany were predominantly Welsh or Irish, and many based themselves on the islands of the Brehat group in the Gulf of St Malo, where there are dedications to the Welsh Saints Illtud, Samson, Gildas and Paulinus.

St Maudez (St Mawes) was born in Ireland and landed at the Island of Ille Modez in the Ille de Brehat – he has many dedications in northern Brittany. He was followed by another Irish – but Wales-based-saint, Brychan of Brycheiniog, although he later returned to south-eastern Wales.

The influence of the Welsh monks is reflected in the fact that the five Bishoprics of Brittany – Dol, St Malo, St Brieuc, Treguier and St Pol de Leon – were all founded by monks from southern Wales.

European River Cultural Provinces

One advantage that Britain enjoyed in the war-torn and unstable post-Roman period was geographical: as an island with a western coastline it was not easy to invade from northern Europe, and consequently the danger came from only one direction – the east.

Continental Europe, however, was in a far more perilous position, for, after the collapse of Roman military power, barbarian tribes rampaged almost unchecked. Unlike Britain, where the Romano-Celtic people could retreat to western strongholds in inaccessible mountain regions, the Christian kingdoms of mainland Europe had no geographical barrier to protect them. The barbarian tribes brought with them pagan beliefs, and this encouraged many local communities to revert to their old ways as a matter of expediency. The Celtic saints, particularly the Irish, were aware of these developments, and took up the task of converting or re-converting people to Christianity throughout Europe. They were also intent on instilling their Celtic Church ideals in place of Roman Church practice and so in their travels they stirred up antagonism from both pagan worshippers and Roman Church authorities alike, which did not make achieving their objectives any easier.

The major inroads to Europe, from Britain and Ireland were made first of all along the western sea routes and then upon the large navigable rivers. Some groups of Celtic saints made a significant contribution to the resurgence of Celtic Christianity in Europe, and whilst they originated from the various cultural provinces of the British Isles, their legacy is distinct enough for these river voyagers to be recognised individually within the movement they created.

Chapter 3

The Western Sea Routes, Celtic and Mediterranean Trade with Britain

'...the Brythons by the headland of Belerium (Land's End) are
unusually hospitable and thanks to their intercourse with foreign
traders have grown gentle in their manner'

Pytheas 330 BC.

The western sea routes used by the Celtic saints from the
fourth to seventh centuries are the ancient trade routes that
linked northern Europe to the Mediterranean, along the
Atlantic shores of Britain, France, Portugal and Spain. The
routes were established during prehistoric times by seafarers,
merchants, adventurers, settlers, and refugees from the early
civilisations of Egypt and other north African and eastern
Mediterranean countries. These are people who voyaged to
the Atlantic shores of western Europe and settled to form
communities large enough to become self sufficient and
eventually leave a permanent record of their stone burial
chambers and circular henges.

These early colonists from the eastern Mediterranean
communities were using implements of flint, slate, stone, bone
and wood. As the Middle East entered the Bronze Age and
their local metalwork industries intensified, the easily worked
reserves of tin, lead, copper and gold available in western
Britain and Ireland attracted even more of these pre-historic
prospectors and traders. They were prepared to undertake the
long and dangerous voyages for the substantial profits that
were to be made, and in doing so linked the Neolithic, stone-

age cultures of northern Europe with the more technologically advanced civilisations of Egypt and the Lebanon.

The first seafaring visitors to the British Isles had voyaged from the south long before the Celts made their appearance in northwest Europe. The British Isles offered many attractions to these early voyagers, for there was mineral wealth; fertile soils coupled with a mild, warm climate favourable for agriculture; and a safe haven for groups of people escaping from war, persecution or famine in their homelands, and seeking new lands to colonise.

The sea routes made use of the prevailing westerly winds and the strong tides of the Atlantic coastline of western Europe. The main routes and their branches stretched from Norway and the western Isles of Scotland, along the whole of western Britain and Ireland, northwest France, the Iberian Peninsula and into the Mediterranean, reaching as far east as the Lebanon and Turkey.

The sea routes were developed over thousands of years to carry all manner of vessels with such diverse cargoes as olive oil, pottery, grain, timber, minerals, cattle and slaves between northern Europe, the Mediterranean and north Africa.

The western sea routes carried not only traded goods, but also cultural practices, philosophy and religious ideas. Most of these were for the mutual benefit of communities at each stage of the voyages, but the western sea routes also carried virulent dangers more deadly than any pirates or raiders: plague, for example, which originated in Egypt in 541, had been carried along the western sea routes and had reached western Britain by 547. This decimated the population and caused a mass exodus from the southwest of the country to Brittany. The western, Celtic areas of the British Isles were more greatly affected than other areas, reflecting their contact with the sea routes along which the virus was carried by unsuspecting crew or passengers. Ireland, also a major destination along the sea routes, was also struck by this outbreak of plague – particularly the more affluent members of society, who were those most likely to come into contact with overseas traders and missionaries. A plague outbreak in Britain had also occurred about four years earlier, possibly from the same source, and Ireland suffered again in 637.

Despite these unwanted invaders, what was most important for the development of north-western Europe was the fact that the western sea routes carried the culture and ideas of people from numerous areas. Many early religious beliefs and cultural practices were introduced to Britain along these routes, the earliest identified being the pagan beliefs of the chambered tomb and henge builders of the early bronze age in around 3,500 BC, culminating in the introduction of Christianity from the Middle East to Britain and Gaul three millennia later.

However, it was the commercial impetus, more than any other factor, which consolidated the western sea routes. Although founded on international trade, these maritime routes then carried early Christianity to Britain and Ireland, where it was to be developed further by the voyaging Celtic saints.

Neolithic Use of the Western Sea Routes

It is likely that sea voyages from the Mediterranean to western Britain had been undertaken from around 4,000 BC. Once out of the Mediterranean, the mariners in their small sailing vessels would stay close to land, perhaps sailing during the day and pulling their boats ashore at night. On steering their ships northwards, they would have the benefit of the prevailing westerly winds on their beam, which would be favourable for taking them along the coasts of Portugal and Spain to northern France and the western coast of Britain, particularly the western peninsulas of Cornwall, southwest Wales, northern Wales, south-western Scotland and Ireland. Sea travel to these western areas of Britain was far easier than the long land trek over the continent. The activities of these early settlers resulted in expansion of the coastal populations of western Britain and its hinterland.

THE WESTERN SEA ROUTES

The new settlements were established along the coastal areas, and then inland along the river valleys and adjoining uplands, with no major contact with the land-based tribes to the east of the country who had made the short sea crossing to the British Isles over the Strait of Dover.

At this time the inhabitants of Britain were still using a stone-age technology, which included wood, bone and other tools. They were hunter-gatherers, and sea-shore communities would collect shellfish to supplement their diets. They were joined by newcomers from the Middle East, where the technology to smelt copper and tin to make bronze had developed, and where urban communities had mastered construction techniques, astronomy and agriculture. These newcomers recognised the valuable natural resources of the land and the seas around western Britain, and whilst some of them were traders, who returned to their homelands leaving in Britain only influences of their culture, others remained as settlers.

There is no suggestion that these settlers made 'non-stop' voyages from the eastern Mediterranean to the British Isles. They probably came in stages, slowly and haltingly, perhaps making their way up the western seaboard of the Atlantic, forming stable settlements, from which they travelled further north, perhaps to escape further pressures that began to impinge on their way of life.

Neolithic Archaeological Evidence

The most striking archaeological evidence of the settlers who voyaged to the British Isles along the western sea routes is found in the distinctive stone burial chambers they erected. These burial chambers are known as dolmens or cromlechs; as well as these megalithic structures, the early settlers also left evidence of their agricultural practices, causeway camps and henges, particularly throughout western Scotland, Ireland, western Cornwall, the coastal areas of southern Wales and northern Somerset that adjoined the Severn estuary, as well as northern Wales and Anglesey.

The dolmens are evidence of an early culture that clearly included religious beliefs in an afterlife, and exercised a significant reverence and ritual for their dead, who they entombed in these chambers.

There are the remains of many dolmens in the coastal areas of western Britain and also other northern European countries along the western sea routes, such as Denmark, northern Germany and north-western France. There are very few dolmens in eastern England. Dolmens are burial chambers constructed of tall upright stones supporting a heavy stone slab, all of which would have been covered with a mound of soil and turf. In this way a secure, sealed tomb was formed. In most cases the soil and roof slab are now long gone and all that remains are the vertical standing stones.

Dolmens offer very significant evidence in identifying cultural links and origins of the societies which built them, for as well as their wide distribution in north-western Europe they are also found in India, Asia and the Middle East in countries such as Iran, Iraq, Jordan, Israel, Palestine and the Lebanon.

In the Old Testament reference is made to the 'iron bed' of the giant King Og (Deut. 3.11). Archaeologists have found this 'iron bed' in Jordan: it is in fact a dolmen constructed of basalt, a very hard, dense, grey-black stone.

The widespread geographical distribution of dolmens is thought to be evidence of mass migration of the population from the Middle East in the period 5,000-3,500 BC. These migrants were perhaps refugees escaping warfare or natural catastrophes, such as drought and famine, in their homelands. They were, in the main, from maritime cultures, for all early civilisations developed along the coast or by the banks and deltas of great rivers such as the Nile, the Euphrates, the Tigris and the Indus. Travelling by sea would be natural to them, and had the advantages of safety, speed and the possibility of travelling great distances. Many of these migrating tribes made use of the western sea routes, and settled in north-western Europe, particularly the western areas of the British Isles. Once these tribes had settled in their new lands and established a self-supporting agricultural regime, they could begin to rebuild their way of life. They could not have immediately commenced the construction of chambered tombs, for these new colonists would have had more pressing needs to fulfil to ensure the initial safety and survival of the community.

When an agricultural surplus was created, labour could be freed and supported for other projects, such as the construction of these large stone burial chambers, and henges. Whilst these structures did eventually appear, it is a matter of conjecture as to how long it took for the community that erected them to establish their ordered, self-sufficient society before they could start construction.

Whilst the great age of these structures is remarkable, what is even more interesting is that the origins of the people who built them can be traced. The form of construction of a dolmen tells us a lot about the route by which the people who built it reached the British Isles. In western Britain there are two main types of Megalithic burial chambers, which are distinguished by different internal designs. Both groups have their origin in the eastern Mediterranean and are known as Passage graves and Gallery graves – the latter also including a distinct, but subsidiary, evolution of Transceptual Gallery graves.

Passage graves are prevalent around the Irish Sea and its approaches. The main landings were on the coasts of Ireland in the Boyne valley area and County Waterford areas and in north Wales on Anglesey and the Llŷn Peninsula. Scotland has examples of Passage graves in the Moray Firth area and they are also found on the south-western coast of Cornwall. The origin of the Passage grave structure may be traced back to Almeria in southeastern Spain and reached the Irish Sea by way of the southwestern coast of Portugal, and the Atlantic route to the Biscay coast of France, to Finisterre, and St Malo in Brittany.

Gallery graves are found in the Carlingford Lough area of

Ireland, where their builders settled to the north of the Boyne group of Passage grave builders, and their origin has been traced back to Sardinia, Corsica, and the Balaeric Islands of Majorca and Minorca, along the Narbonne-Carbilo route to the Loire estuary to southern France, Brittany, and then ultimately, along the Atlantic sea route to Ireland.

In the Loire area a subsidiary type of Gallery grave developed – the Transceptual Gallery grave. People who embarked from this area settled in the Bristol Channel areas of south-eastern Wales, Somerset and south-western Gloucestershire, where they constructed this particular design of chambered tomb. This movement was along the Brittany-Severn estuary stage of the western sea routes.

The identification of the origins of chambered tombs in the British Isles shows that during the Bronze Age period of Britain there were sophisticated communities in contact with each other along the western sea routes, enabling ideas, beliefs and cultural practice to be shared. The Barclodiad y Gawres Gallery graves on Anglesey, constructed in 3,200 BC, have clear similarities to those of the Boyne valley of Ireland. There are also Neolithic cromlechs, such as the rectangular burial chamber close to the village of Y Ffôr near Pwllheli, which display the same construction as those of the east coast of Ireland.

In contrast, the chambered tomb of Capel Garmon, a Passage grave, near Betws-y-coed in the Conwy valley, whilst only a relatively short distance from the Anglesey Gallery graves, has more in common with the Passage grave cromlechs of Breconshire and Glamorgan in southern Wales and those of borders of the Severn Estuary and Cotswolds. All of this later group owe their origin to a culture deriving from Brittany.

Chambered tombs are known in Wales as cromlechs, where there is a total of around 150, and the date of their construction can be established reasonably accurately to around 3,500 BC when, for example, the Gwernvale cromlech in the Usk valley of southern Wales was completed. Henges – circular arrangements of upright standing stones, some of which may have supported headstones and which were probably used for religious and astronomical activities – are not so common, but there are about seventy in Britain. One of the earliest henges may be found at Llandygai near Bangor in northern Wales and has been dated at 3,650-3,390 BC (this date spanning the 3,500 BC calculation of the Usk valley cromlechs).

It can appear incredible that between five and six thousand years ago the cultural ideas and construction techniques of people who set out from lands as far away as modern Lebanon, Jordan or Iraq should establish themselves in the British Isles. The people who made these voyages must have had compelling reasons to undertake such arduous journeys. Subsequent use of the western sea routes by Minoan and then Phoenician traders suggests economic considerations – and there is plenty of evidence of Neolithic trading. For example, some archaeologists now believe that copper from the Great Orme at Llandudno, northern Wales, was mined before the Bronze Age – it was used in its raw state to make copper utensils before the discovery of the bronze manufacturing process – and was traded with locations in France. Also, on the Llŷn Peninsula of northern Wales there is further evidence of Neolithic trading, for some stone axes manufactured there have been found in Gwent, southeast Wales. The continuity of Llŷn as a trading centre on the western sea routes is then confirmed by noting that the stone axes exported to Gwent were manufactured at the same location where, 2,000 years later, a Greek trading ship of the second century BC lost its anchor; it was to be found by divers in 1974. The continuity in cultural and trade links along the western sea routes is a constant theme in the story of Celtic saint voyaging, and recurs at many locations along the Atlantic seaboard.

The activity in the British Isles in the Neolithic period means that a surplus of valuable goods was being produced, and therefore traded, long before the discovery of bronze,

LOCATIONS OF CHAMBERED TOMBS IN WALES

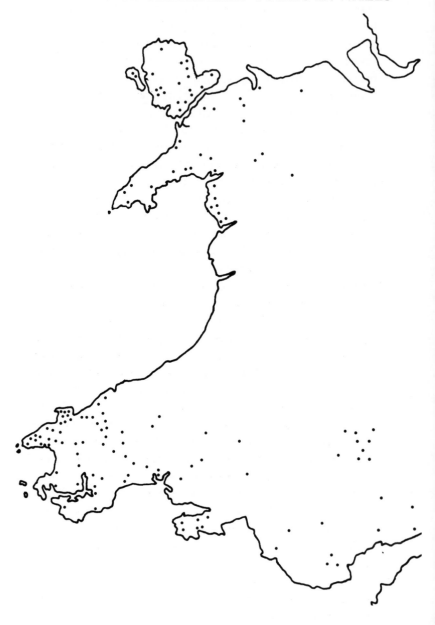

which was to prove the greatest technological development of the era and the greatest stimulus to trade between the Mediterranean countries and northern Europe. The wealth created by the inhabitants of the British Isles and their advantageous location on the western sea routes allowed them to trade as active members of the emerging economic sectors.

Bronze Age Trading along the Western Sea Routes

At the time when the copper mines of northern Wales at the Great Orme and Anglesey were supplying the Bronze Age manufacturers, the dominant international traders of the era were the Minoans, whose culture was founded on the island of Crete.

The most important technical development of the prehistoric era had been the discovery of bronze, probably in Egypt around 3,000 BC. This alloy of tin and copper replaced stone, bone and wood for the manufacture of weapons and implements. Although both tin and copper occur in a natural, usable state, neither is suitable to be used alone in production of tools or weapons, being too soft to retain a sharp edge. When smelted together in the right proportions and at the right temperature, the two metals produce bronze which is hard enough to retain a sharpened edge for use in weapons and tools of all kinds. Bronze and the metals used in its manufacture became highly sought after commodities. The Minoans knew how to make bronze, but unfortunately for them Crete had no deposits of tin or copper, and nor did the island have a population large enough to make production economically viable. The answer was trade – and the British Isles became part of the culture's development.

The Minoans had been leading international traders from around 3,000 BC, and from 2,000 to 1,500 BC they achieved almost total economic and maritime dominance. Although Crete had no great reserves of natural resources nor agricultural land, the Minoans had exceptional cultural and intellectual resources, which attracted an influx of highly skilled artisans, traders and entrepreneurs from other Middle Eastern countries whose abilities developed one of the most important centres of world trade in the ancient world.

The highly skilled and cultured refugees who settled in Crete were probably of Egyptian and Mesopotamian origin fleeing from the politically unstable and war-torn mainland areas of their homelands. They brought with them the most advanced knowledge and skills of astronomy, chemistry, metallurgy, metalworking, construction, commerce, trade, writing and, importantly, shipbuilding. Crete, lying about 250 miles south of the Greek mainland, was ideally situated for maritime trading activities. With a surplus of wine, olives and other agricultural produce, the Minoans started trading for copper from Cyprus, and from Britain when the Cypriot supply became too expensive or difficult to obtain. Tin from south-western Britain became an additional highly valued traded product.

All of the movement of these goods was by sea, and as a consequence the Minoans became seafarers without equal. Their skill at shipbuilding was at the leading edge of the design of large trading vessels and their knowledge of astronomy and mathematics allowed navigation throughout and beyond the Mediterranean. Their fleets traded northwards up the Atlantic coasts of Spain and Portugal, reaching Britain and Ireland. In order to obtain regular supplies, the Minoan traders would have needed a stable culture in the producing areas of the British Isles, and it is likely that there would have been some form of settlement in Britain, perhaps temporary, to oversee and protect Minoan trade interests.

The Minoans declined in around 1,450 BC, possibly due to natural disasters such as earthquakes and inundation by the sea; alternatively they may have been overtaken by a more warlike culture, such as the Mycenaean warrior-based society. But before the culture lost prominence, Minoan supremacy had established the commercial value of the western sea routes and a mutually beneficial trading relationship between the Neolithic society of Britain and the technologically more advanced civilisations of the eastern Mediterranean. This partnership was subsequently developed with Celtic Britain by the Phoenicians.

The Phoenicians

The Phoenicians were initially centred on the eastern Mediterranean, where they occupied a narrow coastal strip of land in the area of modern-day Lebanon. Like the Minoans they were expert seafarers, but additionally they incorporated land-based trading routes to link with major sea routes – for example, their caravan route overland to link the Red Sea to the Mediterranean. These overland connections were also adapted along the western sea routes, particularly along the rugged coasts of Britain and Gaul, where cargo and passengers would be disembarked for overland passage on foot or pony to avoid dangerous voyages around exposed headlands such as Land's End or the Llŷn Peninsula.

The Phoenician trading patterns were recorded by Greek, Roman and Anglo-Saxon writers, and even the authors of the Old Testament of the Bible made quite detailed reference to them.

The Phoenicians were also great explorers, and in around 600 BC King Necho of Egypt commissioned them to circumnavigate the whole of Africa by sea and report back to him. The voyage took three years to complete; the ships were laid up ashore each autumn so that the crew could sow corn to harvest the following spring, when they put to sea once again.

This was an amazing feat of exploration and a superb example of the competence of these shipbuilders, seamen and navigators. A nation capable of constructing ships and providing the organisation and manpower to execute such a voyage had little to fear from regular trips to western Britain.

The Greek astronomer and explorer Pytheas, who

circumnavigated the British Isles in around 330 BC, reported seeing the Phoenician wooden ships sailing amongst the native Celtic leather craft off St Michael's Mount, Cornwall, where they were taking on cargoes of tin for export to the metal manufacturing industries of the Mediterranean. These competent and determined traders voyaged along the whole of the Atlantic coast of Britain, particularly Wales and Ireland, where Mediterranean wine, pottery and manufactured goods could be traded for gold, copper and tin.

This trade along the western sea routes was so important for the Phoenicians that they attempted to monopolise it: in the second and third centuries BC they had complete naval supremacy of the Mediterranean, and there were Phoenician cities guarding the Strait of Gibraltar, where they imposed a blockade to prevent the passage of ships of other nations attempting to enter the Atlantic and the valuable resources of Britain and Ireland.

Celtic and Romano Celtic Traders

Maritime activities did not remain solely dependent on vessels operated by Mediterranean-based fleets, however, for Celtic traders took control of their cargoes, particularly within their own waters. The Veneti tribe, based in southern Brittany, operated, like the Phoenicians, a professional merchant marine. The Veneti were not only traders but also shippers of other tribes' goods, particularly between Britain, Ireland and the continent. Typical traffic would involve the export from Britain of metal such as gold, silver, copper, lead and tin; cattle; leather hides; hunting dogs; and slaves. St Patrick records that his escape to Brittany from slavery in Ireland in around 420 was on a ship exporting hunting dogs. Return voyages of the Veneti ships carried to Britain imports of oil, wine, figs, glass and pottery.

Recent archaeological discoveries of two Celtic bodies preserved in the peat of pre-Roman Ireland give an insight into some aspects of Celtic life. Both are around 2,500 years old. Clonyclavan Man was a young man in his early twenties, about 5'2" in height, who had benefited from a rich diet of meat and vegetables. His body was in such a fine state of preservation that it was possible to determine that his hair had been styled using a pine-resin gel. This particular type of gel could only have been obtained from the Loire area of southwest France. Tacitus wrote of pine-resin gel in around 360 BC. The other body found not too far away is known as Old Croghan Man; he was about 6'6" tall with well-manicured fingernails and found with a rope of hazel around his neck. Both men had suffered violent ritual deaths and had been buried on tribal boundaries, perhaps as sacrifices to fertility gods in order to guarantee good crops. The use of the pine-resin gel in Clonyclavan Man's hair indicates that luxury goods were being traded with the Celtic tribes of south-western France. There were clearly well established direct trading links between the Celtic lands lying on the western sea routes some considerable time before the Romans ventured to northern Gaul and Britain. A product such as hair gel was ideal for trading over great distances because it was lightweight, small but valuable.

Another product of high value and low weight which was traded later was a range of pigments used to make the coloured inks that were utilised to such great effect by literate Celtic monks during the post-Roman Romano-British period. Local plants, animals and minerals, such as iron and oak apples, were used for a range of colours, but some of the more vivid colours required special pigments not available in the British Isles, or even northern Europe. Lapis lazuli was imported from Afghanistan to produce a rich blue ink, whilst pinks and purples were the product of an extract of a particular strain of sunflower growing in the eastern Mediterranean. A bright red was derived from a powder made of crushed insects from southern Europe and north Africa, and a dark blue from the indigo plant of the eastern Mediterranean. These sophisticated items reached the British monasteries along the western trade routes.

LOCATIONS OF IMPORTED
MEDITERRANEAN POTTERY
5th - 7th CENTURY

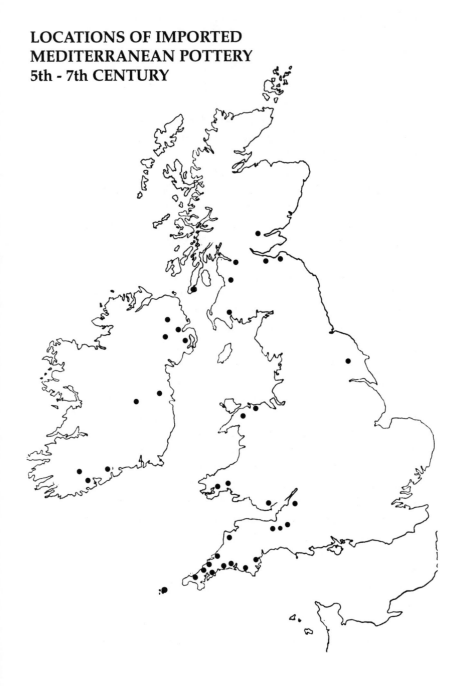

Early navigators wrote of the dangers of the northern waters. In 500 BC the Carthaginian seafarer, Himlico, who had been instructed to voyage to Britain, hinted darkly at the perils that could befall a mariner:

> ...it takes four months from the Pillars to Oestrymnides [Pillars of Hercules/Strait of Gibraltar to the British Isles] on a sea sluggish, blocked with weed and with shoals and sea monsters. There is no wind and a perpetual fog makes navigation impossible.

The British Isles were a valuable trading centre, and it may be that Himlico the Carthaginian might have wanted to deter other traders from venturing along that section of the western sea route.

Homer also contributed to the unfavourable view of the British Isles, when in his Odyssey he writes of 'clouds, mists, the sun not penetrating the day which is so dismal that it is like night hanging over those poor unfortunates who inhabit the land'.

Unlike the Phoenicians, and then the Celts, the Romans favoured land or river routes wherever possible. The Romans had the advantage of a very effective army, and so could provide military escorts for their merchants along overland routes, which would be dangerous for unarmed traders. The Romans were reluctant to make long sea voyages from Britain to the Mediterranean by sailing southwards across the Bay of Biscay, along the coast of Spain and through the Strait of Gibraltar. Their preference, even for transport of copper, gold, silver and tin from western Britain, would be to remain within sight of land. A typical Roman trading route carrying gold from the mines of Wales would commence with the overland journey by horse-drawn wagons along established roads to the south coast of Britain. It is no coincidence that the major Roman roads into Wales were to service the gold mines of Dolaucothi in western Wales and the gold and copper mines of northern Wales. On reaching the southern coast of Britain the wagons were unloaded into coastal barges for a voyage from as far west as St Michael's Mount off Cornwall, making passage eastwards around Hengistbury Head, keeping close to the south coast to Folkestone for transfer to larger vessels and a quick dash across the English Channel to Boulogne to gain the European mainland.

Roman lighthouses at Folkestone and Boulogne were constructed to assist the cross-channel navigators. Merchants would then transfer their cargoes to barges for entry to the Seine, the Loire, the Scheldte or the Rhine, and would then travel overland to the Rhône to finally reach the Mediterranean. These navigational beacons were not available to the voyaging Celtic saints, who did not venture along Britain's southeastern coast but used the western sea routes, particularly when the eastern waters became dominated by Saxon vessels. Consequently, the Celtic saints, even after the fall of the Roman Empire, were still able to utilise the well-established sea routes.

The invasions by Germanic tribes, particularly Saxons during the fifth and sixth centuries, had pushed the British Celts into the western and northern areas of Britain, and so the western sea routes to the Mediterranean or to Brittany were the most convenient and certainly the safest. The shipbuilding, seafaring and navigational skills of the Celtic tribes were the equal, if not superior, to any other nation at the time. The Roman ships, built on Mediterranean principles, were larger than the Celtic vessels but not as robust in withstanding the harsh northern seas.

As well as being competent at undertaking long sea-going voyages, the Celts were also aware, from their trading ventures, of the European river routes which were to be used by the saints in their travels.

There is no shortage of evidence that there was very active sea traffic along the western sea routes long before the age of the Celtic saints, who therefore had at their disposal the means to travel confidently and safely among the various Celtic provinces. The availability of the ships was only one part of the equation – the other essential factor was the ability to plan and execute a passage to a destination far from the departure point, and this required navigation.

Consideration of the background of Mediterranean trade with Britain through Minoan, Phoenician and Greek dynasties emphasises the maritime activity along the western sea routes thousands of years before the unwelcome attentions of Angles, Saxons and other Germanic tribes from northwest Europe. The western sea routes were important not just as a matter of trade, but of shaping culture, awareness and confidence, which fostered a unique society of Britons. This society was energetic and innovative long before the Roman invasion of Britain, and it remained so during and after the Roman occupation – forging a unique Romano-Brythonic culture able to regenerate during the ascendancy of the Celtic saints in the early middle ages.

The political changes of the early middle ages, whilst causing disruption, did not result in total chaos. Long before the successful Roman invasion of 56, BC the Celtic inhabitants of the British Isles had evolved into a well-ordered, industrious and civilised society. Whilst this society was composed of local tribes and chieftains these were, nevertheless, connected to extensive trade and mercantile networks spreading all over Europe and into the Mediterranean. These activities continued throughout the Roman occupation and well into the post-Roman period. These well-established trade routes provided the sea-faring Celtic saints with the means to undertake their voyages around the British Isles and beyond. The monastic orders did not need to acquire boat building or navigational skills, for they had already been long developed and provided by their fellow Celtic craftsmen and seamen.

Chapter 4

EARLY SHIPBUILDING AND NAVIGATION

'The Sea

Look you out
northeastwards
over mighty ocean,
teeming with sea life;
home of seals,
sporting, splendid,
its tide has reached fullness'

(From an Irish Manuscript – *Early Irish Poetry*.
translated by James Carney)

The Celtic saints would not have been effective if they had not been able to travel regularly and safely between the Celtic lands of north-western Europe and also to the religious centres of Rome, Athens and Palestine. In order to do this they needed access to suitable ships for coastal passages, larger vessels for long off-shore voyages and small shallow draught boats capable of being rowed to enable them to navigate the rivers of Britain and continental Europe.

In many cases the saints would have travelled as passengers on trading vessels along established routes, just like ferry passengers today. Some of the saints, however, must have been accomplished seamen in their own right, such as Brendan and his crew of fellow monks, who were not accompanied by professional sailors; or Columbanus, who also travelled almost exclusively by boat with only monks as companions.

An ancient Celtic cross in the ruins of St Ninian's chapel on Sanda Island, which lies between Kintyre, Scotland and Red Bay, Northern Ireland. Sheep Island in the distance.

Skellig Huts on rock islands off the south-western coast of Ireland. These beehive huts were built by 7th century monks at the top of the Great Skellig. Skellig Michael is in the distance.

Séipéilin Ghallaraís, a 9th century prayer house built from dry stones, on Dingle Peninsula, south-western Ireland.

Rathlin Island, off the Antrim's coast in northern Ireland. From here it is only 11 miles to Mull of Kintyre – the shortest voyage between Ireland and Scotland. Cainnech and Brendan crossed from here en route to the Faroe Islands.

A Celtic cross stands in a stone walled field on Inishmore, Aran Islands, western Ireland.

Saint Patrick's Cathedral, Armagh

St Patrick's statue on a hill, Slieve Patrick, near Soul.

St Patricks Grave – he died at Saul and is buried in the graveyard of Down Cathedral.

St Patrick's window

St Patrick's church, Saul – 3 km from Downpatrick is the simple stone church with round tower marking the site of the barn where Patrick first preached in Ireland.

Llanbadrig's church on Anglesey in northern Wales

St Patrick's Causeway ('Sarn Badrig') off the western coast of Wales

*Greenland – from the north of Iceland the Irish monks would see
glimpses of Greenland, or at least the land-based clouds. The autumn
surge of geese flying south would indicate land. East Greenland has a
cold off-shore current keeping the summers cold and so the monks settled
on the west coast which avoids sea ice and has a lusher vegetated
landscape with small trees. Here they could survive on farming similar
to that of Iceland.*

*Angmagssalik area would have been free of sea ice
in the Age of the Saints.*

Sunset over Angmagssalik.

Faroe Islands – a group of 18 islands, visited by many Irish saints, particularly Brendan and Cainnech who described 'the Paradise of the Birds' and 'Island of Sheep'.

Iona cathedral from the sound.

Isle of Mull. Visited by Columba and many other Celtic Saints taking christianity to the Pictish tribes.

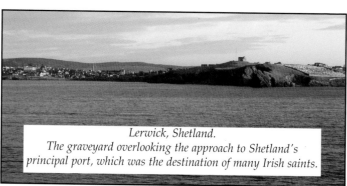

*Lerwick, Shetland.
The graveyard overlooking the approach to Shetland's principal port, which was the destination of many Irish saints.*

Lindisfarne Island, the harbour and castle.

A Senegot – a traditional fishing boat of the Golfe de Morbihan in southern Brittany.

*St Curig's church and oratory at the beach,
Ploumanac'h Brittany where the saint first
landed and preached when he crossed the sea
from Wales; St Curig's maritime connections
are mirrored in his stained glass window at
Llangrannog's church, Wales*

The Breton church and the sea – the connections go back over the centuries to the Age of the Celtic saints.

St Malo sailed to Brittany from Wales and established his church where the busy port stands today.

The Bretons still commemmorate their Celtic saints with traditional 'Pardon' processions

Celtic saints are connected to many sailors' churches along the Celtic coast:

Santa Barba, Roscoff, Brittany

St Stinian's chapel, Tenby

St David's, Barmouth

*St Tudwal's island West, off the
northern Welsh coast*

*St Tudwal's cathedral, Treguier,
Brittany*

Images of St Tudwal at Treguier cathedral.

St Cybi sailed from Cornwall to establish Christian communities at

Holyhead (Caergybi) on Anglesey

Llangybi, Eifionydd - where Ffynnon Gybi (his well) was an important pilgrim centre until very recent times

*St Teilo sailed from Wales to establish Christian communities at
Dol and Lanelo in Brittany*

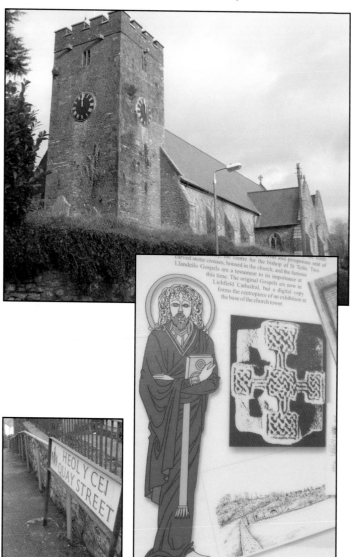

*Llandeilo Fawr, Carmarthenshire, with the lane winding down from the
'llan' to the quay on the river Tywi.*

St Crannog (Carantoc) sailed from Brittany to establish Christian communities at Llangrannog in south-western Wales

Llangrannog's church

Govan, also from Brittany, had his hermit cell in St Govan's cliffs, Pembrokeshire

St Non (the mother of Dewi – St David of Wales)
came from Ireland

St Non's well, Pembrokeshire

St Non's window at Llan-non

St Non's chapel

St Ffraid (St Briget) also sailed from Ireland and is connected to many churches in Wales

Beuno is probably the saint who has the most churches consecrated to him in northern Wales. Nearly all of these are very close to the shoreline.

St Ffraid's church – Eglwys Santes Ffraid, Llan-non

Maen Beuno at Clynnog Fawr

Beuno's church at Clynnog-fawr, north-western Wales

Beuno's church at Trefdraeth on the Isle of Anglesey

Among the sacred islands of the Welsh coast are:

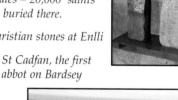

Ynys Enlli, north-western Wales (Bardsey Island). Christians were carried there for burial from all over western Wales – 20,000 'saints' are reputed to be buried there.

Early Christian stones at Enlli

St Cadfan, the first abbot on Bardsey

St Cwyfan's church, Anglesey

Mwnt church, Ceredigion – one of the burial sailing points to Bardsey

Llanddwyn - St Dwynwen's island, Anglesey, the patron saint of Welsh lovers

Caldey island –
Ynys Bŷr, named after St Pŷr
– Pembrokeshire

St Tysilio's island, Anglesey

Ynys Seiriol, named after St
Seiriol, but known in English as
Puffin Island

St Seiriol's church and monastery,
Penmon

Ynys Dewi – St David's island (also known as Ramsey Island),
Pembrokeshire

Dewi Sant - St David of Wales – is commemorated throughout Wales and also in churches in Brittany, Ireland and western England

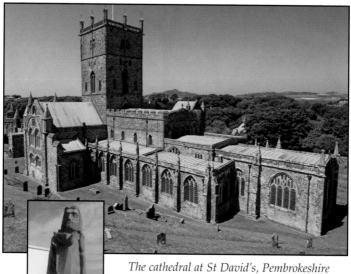

The cathedral at St David's, Pembrokeshire

Dewi's statue by the new church at Tywyn, Meirionnydd

Dewi's statue in Llanddewi Brefi

Dewi's church at Llanddewi Brefi, the site of one of his famous miracles

Sites connected to Dewi in Brittany – Capel Sant Divi (St David's chapel) at Ploneour-Menez; Sant Divi's well and statue at Dirinonn.

St David's church at Moreton-on-Marsh, western England

Trillo's cell on the beach at Llandrillo-yn-Rhos

St Danwg's church in the sand dunes, Meirionnydd

St Daron's church above the beach in Llŷn

A navigational scene at Llanaber's church above the shore, Meirionnydd

Whether the saints were voyaging as passengers or as commander and crew, they needed as basic requirements sound, seaworthy vessels, people with the knowledge of how to sail them, and the knowledge of how to safely navigate not only to their destination but also to return home.

Like Christianity, whose origins lie in the Middle East but which was adapted to the particular needs of a western European population converting from paganism, shipbuilding and navigation skills also had origins in, and developed out of, the Middle East.

Shipbuilding

From Reeds to Wood

The first ships are to be found among the boat-builders of the world's oldest civilisation, the Egyptians, who built their ships out of reeds. They also exported these reeds, or papyrus, to other countries bordering the eastern Mediterranean, where the Phoenicians and the Hittites developed their own boat-building industries. It was in this area that the advantage of timber for the construction of ships was first realised.

The area of the Mediterranean which is present-day Lebanon once had huge cedar forests. This timber was easily worked and split from logs into planks. The Phoenicians were the first to use their home-grown cedar for the construction of ships, particularly as this had a tremendous cost advantage for them. They had built their first ships from papyrus, but had to import this from Egypt at considerable expense. As they developed woodworking skills they found that cedar, in addition to being available locally, was a far superior, stronger and more durable shipbuilding material.

Eventually the Egyptians, who wished to keep pace with technological advances, were forced to import timber from the Lebanon to satisfy their own boat-building industry. To obtain cedar, the Egyptians traded cotton, building stone such as granite from their quarries on the upper Nile, and copper. Trade with the Phoenicians was so extensive that as records indicate, the port of Byblos had one harbour specially set aside for vessels trading with Egypt.

The transition from reeds to timber probably occurred around 3,000 BC; from then on ships around all parts of the Mediterranean were constructed of planks fastened together by pegs, joints and rope lashings. This form of construction was exported to northern Europe: the Egyptian method of peg and beam construction has been found in the remains of one of Britain's oldest boats, which was discovered at North Ferriby in Yorkshire and dated to around 950 BC.

Despite this radical change in boat-building materials, the design of the vessels of that time did not change. Although wood replaced reeds as a means by which buoyancy was maintained, the ship retained its high upswept bow and stern which, through extensive usage on long voyages, had been proven to provide excellent sea-keeping qualities. As discussed later, these features were retained in the construction of the Celtic craft of northern Europe.

Over the next thousand years or so, the demands made on the once vast cedar forests of the Lebanon resulted in an increasing scarcity and rising cost of that timber. Cedar was gradually replaced by pine obtained from northern Europe,

EGYPTIAN REED BOAT

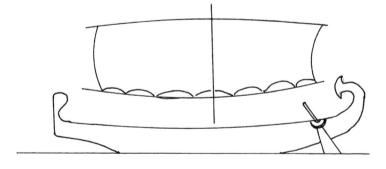

and eventually oak became the preferred shipbuilding material because of its strength, durability and availability. The use of oak continued well into the nineteenth century, by which time this was almost universally used in the construction of sailing ships. The decks of the ships were usually of fir planks, and trade with Egypt provided good quality cotton used for sails and ropes.

Before the demise of reed ships it had been recorded by the Egyptian geographer and mathematician Eratosthenes that reed boats, similar to those that plied the river Nile and its delta, had sailed as far as Sri Lanka and then continued to the mouth of the river Ganges. The latter part of the voyage took twenty days at an average speed of around three knots. This allowed a daily distance of seventy-two nautical miles – a respectable achievement for a heavily laden cargo vessel five thousand years ago.

Wooden boats in the British Isles

The remains of heavy timber-planked boats dating from around 1,000-900 BC have been found around the British coast, from Caldicot and Goldcliff in southern Wales to the Humber estuary of Yorkshire. These boats were up to twelve metres in length and were constructed of wooden planks that had been cut and shaped by metal tools. The planks of the hull were fixed together by wooden wedges, pegs and cleats, as well as being stitched by supple branches of yew and willow.

These were probably flat-bottomed estuary boats and had been built almost a thousand years before the Roman invasion of Britain, showing that a skilled boat-building trade was well established there. The boats had been built by the progressive fixing together of planks side by side – there were no ribs or frames to hold them together. Over the next three to four hundred years the fixing together of the planks, usually of oak, became more permanent with the use of wooden pegs or nails, but the hull was still a shell construction. It was built from the centre outwards, with the planks being fastened to each other.

With the development of Iron Age technology around 150 BC, there was a radical change in the way ships were built. Wooden-planked ships started to be built around a frame comprised of a strong central keel supporting ribs or frames to which the planks were fixed by iron nails. This allowed the construction of stronger sea-going ships capable of transporting heavy or bulky cargoes.

Celtic Ships, Boats and Maritime Activity

The Iron Age Celtic people of northern Europe were aware of the geography of the Mediterranean and the adjoining lands. They had the navigational skills needed to make trading ventures to these areas, and just as importantly were able to find their way back. They also had the boat-building skills to provide their own vessels. There were a variety of different designs and constructions available to them depending on the use to which the vessels were to be put.

Boats of leather

In 320 BC the Greek astronomer and explorer Pytheas wrote in his book *On the Ocean (Peri tou Okeanon)* of seeing boats made of hide sailing off southwest England. This confirmed earlier observations by the Latin poet Rufus Festus Aviensis whose Ora Maritima of the fourth century BC described:

> ... the people of the Oestrymnides [British Isles] sailing boats freely on rough seas teeming with sea monsters. They do not make hulls of pitch pine, or shape wooden keels in the usual way – but were hides stitched together so that the boat sailed on the sea on leather.

Both Pytheas and Rufus Aviensis must have found the hide boats seen around the British Isles unusual and worthy of comment and their observations confirm that during the Bronze Age wooden ships from the Mediterranean were sharing the coastal waters of the British Isles with native boats of leather hulls.

The building of leather boats in the west of the British Isles was still in use during the age of Celtic Christianity some eight hundred years after Pytheas' comments, when in AD 563 St Columba recorded his passage from Howth, near Dublin, to the Scottish Isle of Iona in a leather boat (a curragh) rowed by twelve monks.

Another Irish monk, St Brendan of Clonfort, also voyaged in a leather boat with oars and sails from southwest Ireland far into the north Atlantic. The boats described by Columba and Brendan are very similar to the curraghs still built and used today off the wild Atlantic coast of southern Ireland. There is still a tradition of building leather and canvas boats in south-western Ireland and also in western Wales, where smaller, rounded coracles powered by a single oar can be seen on the rivers Teifi, Taf and Tywi. The coastal voyages around Cardigan Bay by St Tysilio were also undertaken in boats made of hide in the curragh style. The materials used in the construction of these leather boats do not lend themselves to preservation and so there are no archaeological remains available for study. The construction of modern curraghs gives an indication of the likely structure of the early boats and there are manuscripts and woodcuts which also give a pictorial impression. However, the most important evidence for the design and structure of Celtic leather boats comes from the remarkable gold model of a ship found in a hoard at Broighter on Lough Foyle,

Early Irish boat - 8th century carving on stone pillar of cross, Bantry Bay Ireland

Northern Ireland. The hoard of seven objects, dated to between the first century BC and first century AD, comprises a large gold torque, two smaller gold torques, two necklaces and two gold models – one of a cauldron and one of a fully equipped ship. The 'Broighter ship' is a detailed model of a hide boat, with nine cross benches, each for two rowers, eighteen oars, a rowlock, steering oar, and a mast and a yard for hoisting a square rigged sail. There are also three barge poles and a grappling hook. The dimensions of the model indicate that the vessel it represents was in the region of twelve to fifteen metres long.

Boats of hide were extremely seaworthy, easily rowed and capable not only of making estuary and coastal passages but also venturing offshore, as demonstrated in the 1970s by the explorer Tim Severin, who sailed far into the north Atlantic in a leather curragh based on the design of the craft that St Brendan had used. They were ideal for passenger transport but of limited use as trading vessels. It would not take much imagination to visualise the damaging effect a cargo of

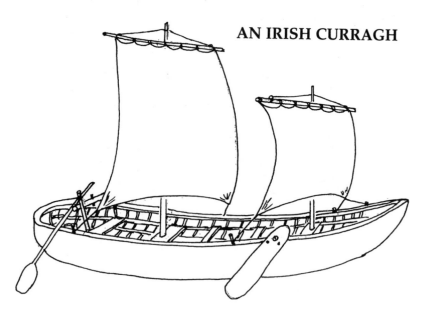

AN IRISH CURRAGH

livestock such as horses or cattle would have had on a lightly framed boat with a leather hull. There was also a limitation to the size of a boat constructed this way, and the shipment of heavy cargoes such as tin or lead ingots, barrels of wine or oil, would require much larger and more durable ships.

Celtic trading ships and their construction

The Iron Age Celtic seagoing ships were impressive, perhaps even more so than their Mediterranean counterparts. Julius Caesar was certainly impressed on encountering the ships of the Celtic Veneti tribe of northwestern Gaul. He described these vessels as having a high bow and stern with a flat keel and strong sides of oak planks fastened to massive cross beams and ribs with iron nails. These boats also had anchors and chains of iron and hide sails. Such Celtic ships had been developed to be able to withstand the severe weather, fierce currents and vast tidal range encountered on the western

A CELTIC TRADING SHIP WITH IRON FITTINGS ANCHOR AND CHAINS.

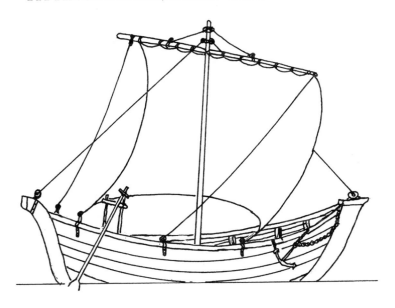

shores of Britain and mainland Europe. These were conditions that the shipbuilders of the Mediterranean did not have to contend with, and so there were distinct differences between the shipbuilding styles of the northern European Celtic boat-builders and their Mediterranean counterparts.

The Romans subsequently incorporated aspects of Celtic designs in their own vessels, and examples of these Romano-Celtic ships have been found at Magor, southern Wales, in the remains of a heavily constructed planked vessel, possibly a barge, over eleven metres in length. Other examples have been found at Blackfriars, London and at St Peter Port, Jersey. The Blackfriars boat, with a length of 18.5 metres, was larger than the Magor find and could carry a cargo of up to fifty tonnes. This vessel was also decked and had a lined hold, the hull being constructed of heavy nailed planks. The St Peter Port boat had refinements of a deck cabin with fired-clay roof-tiles, a hearth and cooking utensils, indicating that long voyages were catered for. Perhaps careless use of the hearth sealed the fate of the St Peter Port ship, which shows evidence of having caught fire and burning down to the waterline before sinking, with its cargo of wine, into the harbour.

The Romans also left depictions of their ships in mosaics and on coinage – much of it being minted in Britain - which indicates the importance placed on the Roman British fleet, the Classis Britannica. The most interesting example of this coinage was produced in the period after AD 287, when the admiral of the fleet, Marcus Carausius, seized Britain and ruled the province for six years. Whilst he was admiral, Carausius, whose duty was to protect Britain from Germanic pirates, was already under suspicion of allowing the pirates to carry out their raids and then intercepting them when they were returning home carrying valuable booty, which he confiscated for his own use. Having seized control of Britain, Carausius was safe from retribution from Rome because he had retained control of the Channel fleet. He was untouchable from a military point of view because no army from mainland Europe had the means to reach Britain. He minted and issued new coins bearing the title IMP[erator] and AUG[ustus] and in 290, when he appointed himself Caesar, added the title C to his coinage. Coins of Carausius also bore depictions of a planked ship with oars and also a mast and yard for a sail representing a capital ship of the Channel fleet.

Carausius, who was a Belgic Gaul with possible British or Manx links, was eventually murdered by his finance minister, Allectus, who then took the title of Caesar for himself, issuing coins in Britain bearing his head and also introducing a new bronze coin known as a quinarius with a galley on the reverse. Several designs of ships were minted on his coins and one depicts a typically Celtic hull profile with a raised prow and stern. The rule of Allectus was also short-lived, possibly because, unlike Carausius, his background as finance minister did not earn him the loyalty of the Channel fleet. In 296 AD, Roman soldiers loyal to the

ROMANO CELTIC TRADING SHIP

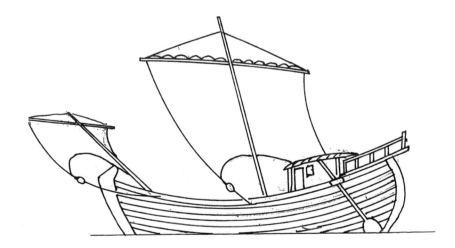

Emperor landed on the south coast and a fleet sailed up the Thames, disembarking further troops who defeated and killed the usurper. The control of shipping was evidently a dominant factor in the rule of Britain.

Construction of Celtic wooden ships

The shipwrights who built the wooden planked hulls of Celtic trading ships, such as those operated by the Veneti tribe, used what is known as a clench, or clinker construction. This is a boat-building technique which has been used in north-western Europe since the early middle ages until the present day. Although it is now used rarely for large vessels, there are many small harbours or creeks around the coastline of the British Isles where a clench-built boat is likely to be found on a mooring or pulled up on a beach. The design is so enduring that some simulated 'clinker' (clench) boats are constructed out of glass-reinforced plastic. The distinctive visual feature of this design is that each of the individual planks making up the hull overlaps its neighbour. This makes a very strong hull construction and is also thought to result in a drier boat, for waves striking the hull are deflected away by the exposed, downwards-facing plank edges. The clench-built hull also has disadvantages when compared to contemporary boat-building techniques and materials, because it results in a relatively heavy boat requiring substantially more timber to complete. However these were not problems for Romano-British or Celtic shipbuilders, who had ample supplies of good-quality oak, and benefited from a culture that nurtured skilled craftsmen in many disciplines.

Clench construction required craftsmanship, but not a great deal of calculation, and could be completed by a relatively small team within a typical Celtic community. The construction of a clench-built boat commenced with the laying down of a straight oak keel to which upright pieces of oak timber were morticed to form the upswept prow (stem) and stern. A groove was then cut into each side of the keel for its entire length, continuing up into the stem and sternposts. The first two planks were fastened into the grooves either side of the keel, to form the lowest planks in the hull – known as the garboard strakes. Further planks were then added, each one overlapping the preceding plank. At a midway point along the keel a transverse mould in the shape of the anticipated hull cross-section would be fixed to form a template along which the hull planks could be laid. Each plank was fastened to its neighbour by long iron nails, which protruded through the planks and whose ends were bent over or 'clenched' to hold them permanently in place. In order to hold the planks in position while the iron nails were being driven, the boat builders used large wooden clamps, like giant-sized clothes pegs, made out of naturally curved branches of wood selected from grown timber.

As the hull was progressively taking shape, cross beams and floors were added, these too fixed with iron nails to the keel and hull planking. Wooden pegs known as trenails were also used to keep the ship's structure tightly fastened. These trenails, or dowels, were made by hammering a length of oak though a round iron collar into which a sharp edge had been cut. This provided consistently rounded pegs, which were driven into holes that had been drilled into the planks and frames by an auger. The wooden pegs would be a tight fit and would tighten further as they became wet and expanded when the boat was launched.

The boat would be fitted with cross benches for rowing, and larger vessels could be decked over with removable hatches providing access to a lined hold. A solid timber mast and a single horizontal spar would support a sail stitched from thin and supple hide. Ropes were woven from flax, and where strength was required, such as for an anchor, iron chains and fittings were made.

Vessels such as these could be constructed from any sheltered area of land adjacent to navigable water, whether a river or the sea, by a fairly small workforce. The master builder would employ two or three men to form planks of the required dimensions by splitting a felled oak using wedges hammered in along its length. These roughly split planks would then be faired smooth with an axe or adze.

A skilled shipwright would approve the planks and then clamp and fit them to assemble the hull. Iron nails would be made by the blacksmith, a highly regarded man in Celtic society, and a skilled craftsman who also manufactured weapons, agricultural and domestic equipment and the shipwright's tools. The driving of the iron nails through the planks and their clenching was a two-man job – one on the inside bending and cutting the ends of the nails and the other outside with a hammer or heavy weight to keep the nails held in tight until they were clenched.

Clench-built vessels were very strong and could take rough treatment. Even when damaged, repairs were straightforward and so the owners could expect a long working life from their vessels.

Unlike the early leather-hulled curraghs and coracles, which have left no physical remains to be examined, examples of wooden-planked ships of the early middle ages have occasionally been found preserved where they had been abandoned in the mud of a former estuary – or, in the case of the most noteworthy example in Britain, preserved in a seventh-century burial mound at Woodbridge, Suffolk. Known as the 'The Sutton Hoo ship', it is an Anglo-Saxon vessel of about twenty-seven metres in length and a beam (maximum width) of 4.5 metres. The timber planking of this boat had rotted away but had left clearly defined imprints of its clench construction and iron nails in the surrounding clay.

River boats

There are a number of illustrations and also depictions on coins of wooden boats used to navigate the major rivers of Europe. These boats are also of clench construction but have a different hull shape, for they were barge-like and not primarily sailing boats, but propelled by oars or hauled by a towrope from the river bank. They were more likely to have a shallow draft, flat bottom and a straight keel so that they could be dragged over gravel shoals, and many illustrations show a line of men heaving on a tow line passing over their shoulders as they trudge upstream pulling their boat against the current. Neither did these river boats have the upswept prow or stern of the sea-going vessels, for there would not be high waves to threaten them – a low, unobstructed barge-type construction would also make it easier to employ a tow rope without getting it snagged on unnecessary structures or ornamentation.

Sails

There is very little archaeological information about the rig, or sail configuration, of Celtic ships. Julius Caesar commented on the use of sails made of stitched supple hides and presumably he considered this noteworthy because they were different to Roman sails, which were made of linen. He did not comment on the rig or set of the sails and so by inference saw nothing unusual, leading us to suppose that the rig of Celtic ships was little different to that of Roman ships, about which there is a reasonable amount of historical information.

The earliest depiction of a sailing ship was found on pottery dated to 2,900 BC in Egypt, and shows a square-rigged vessel. The sail was a square shape and hung from a horizontal spar affixed towards the top of a single mast. This rig is also indicated on the Celtic gold model ship found at Broighter, which clearly shows a single mast and one horizontal spar. There are also many pictures of Roman trading ships flying a square sail, but the rig evolved to incorporate two triangular sails hoisted above the main square sail and also an 'artemon' – a second, smaller square sail flown from a bowsprit and spar projecting over the bow of the vessel. This rig would have given an improved sailing performance, and is likely to have been adapted by Celtic boat builders: it is the nature of ships that they sail to foreign destinations and mingle with ships of other nations, where improvements of designs are noted, discussed and copied by their masters and owners.

One disadvantage of the square-rigged sail is that while it is suitable when the ship is sailing downwind (in the same direction as the wind), it is not efficient in sailing into the wind. This would have been a disadvantage for Celtic saints voyaging in the Irish Sea or along the west coast of Britain, because the prevailing winds and the geography would have required a significant amount of windward sailing. The trade with the Mediterranean would have given the opportunity for Celtic mariners to see vessels with a 'lateen' rig, in which the horizontal main spar of the square sail is replaced with a steeply sloping wooden spar supporting a triangular sail. This could be rigged on a heavy wooden clench-built vessel or on the leather-hulled craft favoured by the Welsh and Irish mariners. This rig was most likely used on these smaller vessels and would have given considerable manoeuvrability and versatility to the voyaging saints of the Irish Sea and Bristol Channel, enabling faster and more frequent passage-making, particularly of lightly laden ships carrying only passengers.

Despite the skills of ship builders, sailing masters and navigators, the voyages around the coastline of the British Isles were perilous. One of the dangers faced by seafaring traders voyaging to western Britain is suggested by the lead anchor found in Bardsey Sound, between Bardsey Island and the mainland of Llŷn, in northern Wales. Embellished with the god Venus and dated to the second century BC, this was most likely from a Greek trading vessel making for the copper mines of Anglesey or the Great Orme, both of which were productive at that time. This anchor probably tells a story of catastrophe, for Bardsey Sound is not an anchorage but a sea passage, which at unfavourable times of wind and tide can be treacherous even to a modern sailing ship with a powerful diesel engine. It is easy to imagine the scenario of the crew of the Greek vessel finding themselves unable to make way against an unfavourable tide race, and desperately dropping their anchor in an attempt to prevent themselves being swept onto a rocky lee shore. The location of the anchor on the sea bed suggests that the attempt was probably unsuccessful, perhaps due to the anchor chain snapping under the strain. It is possible to take a more optimistic view and suppose that the anchor and chain held, saving the ship and its crew, but that the tackle had become so embedded in the rocky bottom that it could not be recovered and had to be abandoned as the ship sailed away.

Navigation

Mediterranean navigation

Mediterranean navigators such as Pytheas relied heavily on astro-navigation techniques, using the stars at night and the sun during the day. The Mediterranean navigators had no tidal streams to influence the course of their vessels, in contrast to the Celtic navigators of northern Europe, particularly around the British Isles and Gaul, who rarely had clear skies to allow them to take a regular 'fix' and also had to allow for the effects of some of the highest tidal ranges in the world, which created tidal streams or currents against which a sailing ship could be powerless. There were therefore significant differences between the navigation techniques used by these two sets of seafarers.

The sun and the stars

Modern navigators have available to them accurate charts giving a mass of information to enable voyages to be safely planned and executed. They also have instruments such as a magnetic compass, a sextant, a radio and other electronic means of navigation, including satellite-based global positioning systems (gps). The magnetic compass was not available during the Age of the Saints because it did not reach Europe until there was access to Chinese science in the later Middle Ages.

There is a tendency to think that Celtic and Mediterranean seafarers of the early middle Ages had nothing to guide them, but in fact they did have rudimentary charts of the coast and an understanding of tides, weather patterns, basic navigation techniques and seamanship. Early navigators could also use the sun, moon, planets and stars to calculate the position of the vessel and the course to steer to arrive at its destination. When Thor Hyerdahl undertook his transatlantic voyage in the Ra I, a reed boat constructed on traditional Egyptian lines, he commented that navigation would have been very easy for the seafarers who made the same voyage many thousands of years before him. He made the simple observation that every day the sun set directly ahead of the bow of the vessel.

Similarly, a navigator leaving the Mediterranean today and following the Pole Star would make a landfall on the shores of Ireland. The northern hemisphere skies were slightly different in previous ages, for two thousand years ago Cassiopeia, a distinctive constellation, was below the horizon and could not be seen, and even the North Star, Polaris, was not as useful as it is today because it was thirteen degrees away from its present position. Consequently there was no Pole Star to guide the early mariners, but they could use Kochab, which, at that time, was about seven and a half degrees away from the magnetic Pole.

These are simple examples of astro-navigation in its most basic form, but the ancient navigators were actually far more sophisticated in their calculations. They knew that the sun and the stars moved through the sky in such a well-ordered way that they were reliable. The planets were not trusted because they appeared to wander around the heavens in a random fashion. Mathematicians and astronomers did eventually learn to predict the movement of these 'wandering stars' but in the early days of astro-navigation they had to be disregarded.

Those who supervised the construction of stone henges

and other similar structures four thousand years ago had sufficient astronomical knowledge to enable them to determine the precise site and alignment of tombs and temples with the sun, and this information would have been available to the seafarers and merchants whose trade with distant countries was of immense economic importance.

The records of the first seafarers to trade regularly with Britain – the Phoenicians and Minoans – are lost, but the Greeks left a wealth of written detail about the seafarers' use of astro-navigation techniques long before the discovery of the magnetic compass.

Although Homer's Odysseus, 'the bald headed, talkative seaman', was a fictional character, the technical descriptions of his long voyages by ship, and the sailing skills that he and his crew employed, are undoubtedly accurate and based on the knowledge of the day in 1,200 BC. The narrative of Odysseus frequently refers to his observations of the stars to enable him to keep his vessel on course and to tell him where he and his companions were.

Odysseus and other navigators knew, for example, that to reach a certain destination they should always keep the constellation of Orion the Hunter on the right-hand side of their ship. Orion can occasionally dominate the southern sky because of its distinctive outline and the brightness of its main stars. Orion the Hunter wears a belt composed of three closely spaced stars which point down to Sirius. Sirius is the brightest star in the sky but not always seen from the northern hemisphere, as it can be below the horizon for part of the year.

In Greek mythology Orion was the hunter and Sirius was his dog. In one of the stories in The Odyssey, Odysseus wishes to set off on a voyage 'before the Dog had set'. The Dog Star was an important navigational star for Greek seamen.

Odysseus knew that all of the stars wheeled around the sky but only the Great Bear (also known as The Plough) did not 'bathe in the ocean's stream'. The Great Bear was always visible in the northern hemisphere and never set during the night. Odysseus saw that as it moved across the sky it would graze the water when observed from the Nile Delta, but when the ship was off Greece it would clear the horizon by the full width of his fist held at arm's length in front of him. When Odysseus' ship was at a point halfway along the important and well-used trade route between Greece and the Nile Delta, the Great Bear would pass above the horizon at the height of two fingers when at its lowest point. (Perhaps some motorists who we see gesturing with two fingers and a fist are unwittingly using the basics of this time-honoured method of navigating.)

The knowledge of the relative positions of these well-known constellations was of great assistance to ocean navigators, and gave them assurance that not only would they be reaching their destination, but that they would also be able to return. These early techniques were later refined by others, such as the Arabs, who replaced the fist and fingers technique with the notched wooden blocks and knotted strings of the kabal, which was one of the first navigational instruments.

The Phoenicians recorded that during their circumnavigation of Africa, the sun was on the right-hand side of their boat when they rounded the southernmost point of land. They were clearly making repeated sightings of the position of the sun to assist their expert navigation.

The Greeks believed that knowledge was to be shared and that theories and discoveries were to be openly debated, not only with other philosophers but with the public. To be a philosopher in the days of early Greek civilisation was to be a member of a profession by which one would earn one's living. It was not a religious post or one that was dependent on the financial support of a government department or royal patronage. A philosopher would earn his living from the translation of his intellectual discovery into a practical, economic application. The philosopher who was seen to be successful in open debates would be more likely to attract students prepared to pay fees for their education.

This open and competitive approach to the quest for knowledge resulted in the Greeks providing major astronomical observations and practical applications to others, but it is also the Greek writers who complain most about the climate of northern Europe, particularly the cloudy skies and long periods of sea mist, because these features obscured the sun by day and the stars by night, making astro-navigation impossible.

Pytheas – his voyage around Celtic Britain.

One Greek ship that returned safely to its home port was the vessel commanded by the astronomer Pytheas, who gave a first account of the earliest recorded circumnavigation of the British Isles. Pytheas, who had been a student of Aristotle, had an inquisitive and adventurous nature, and combined his land-based astronomical achievements with skills as a seaman, navigator and scientific observer. Before leaving on his great voyage from the Mediterranean into the unknown world of the high northern latitudes, Pytheas had already demonstrated to his contemporaries that the Pole Star, although very useful to Greek navigators in indicating the direction of north, was not actually at the Pole. It is possible that one of the objectives of his voyage was to establish by personal observation the conclusion he had reached in theoretical and mathematical terms. Another motive may have been his curiosity about the northern Celtic lands described to him by seafarers and merchants who brought from there, to his home port of Massalia, such a wide variety of finely manufactured goods, amber, tin and gold in exchange for Mediterranean wine and pottery.

In 330 BC Pytheas set out from the Greek colony of Massalia (now Marseilles) on a voyage as far to the north as he could reach. It is not known whether the expedition left the Mediterranean at the port of Narbo (Narbonne) to take the overland route to enter the Bay of Biscay at Bordeaux, or undertook the long voyage through the Strait of Gibraltar and around the Atlantic coast of Portugal and Spain. From Massalia to the mouth of the Gironde in the Bay of Biscay would be a journey of 3,200 kilometres by sea but only 500 kilometres by the overland route. Also at that time the Phoenicians were imposing a blockade of the Strait and passage of a Greek vessel may have been difficult. These factors suggest that the overland passage would have been favoured, but it would mean that on reaching Bordeaux Pytheas would have had to purchase or charter a ship to take him to the northern latitudes that he wished to study. This factor alone makes it likely that he would have wished to retain the use of the vessel in which he had departed Massalia, for it would have undoubtedly been specifically chosen for its sea-keeping qualities and provisioned with supplies and equipment required for an arduous voyage into the unknown. Whatever route taken for this initial part of the voyage, it is known that Pytheas landed in the region of Ushant, off Brittany, where he recorded his latitude. From here he made a direct passage to 'Antivestaeum sive Belerium Promi', Lands End – noting the distance travelled and probably navigating by the sun.

Pytheas was skilled at calculating the latitude of any position by use of a gnomon, a portable vertical stick or column, the shadow of which was used to fix a meridian enabling him to note in the ship's log the latitude of every stage of his voyage. These navigational records meant that the location of the British Isles could be accurately plotted on maps for the first time. This does not mean that Pytheas 'discovered' Britain, for his account describes the already well-established trading procedures of the Phoenician merchants who met native Britons on St Michael's Mount, off Cornwall, for exchange of Mediterranean manufactured goods and produce for Cornish tin. Pytheas also landed in Cornwall and was impressed with the local people, noting that 'the Brythons by the headland of Belerium are unusually hospitable and thanks to their intercourse with foreign traders have grown gentle in their manner'.

He recorded how the tin prepared for export to Mediterranean lands was mined and smelted by the Britons, and was then hammered into knuckle-sized lumps for transportation (he is probably referring to a knuckle of bone from an ox – not a human finger). At low tide the tin was taken out to St Michael's Mount on wooden wagons pulled by ponies.

From Cornwall Pytheas continued his voyage along the south coast of Britain, through the Straits of Dover and then, once again, northwards. The ship reached the northernmost shore of the British Isles by keeping to this course, but then sailed on for a further six days in the quest to reach the North Pole. Pytheas was prevented from achieving this objective by the ice shelf of the Arctic, but he probably reached Iceland, which he called 'Thule'.

Pytheas had difficulty in understanding and describing the huge ice-bergs and pack ice that he encountered. He tried to convey an understanding of what he had seen and observed that 'around Thule there is neither sea nor air but a mixture like a sea lung in which earth and air are suspended'. He described the sea as being 'curdled'.

Despite the meticulous nature of his observations, this description of the Arctic Circle was the most difficult, for it concerned a previously unknown phenomenon. It also proved to be the most contentious part of his narrative: his description of the Arctic ice was not believed by his fellow philosophers on his return to Greece.

After leaving the Arctic Circle Pytheas sailed south to rejoin the coastal waters of the British Isles where he continued his circumnavigation in an anti-clockwise direction. His exploration along the Atlantic coast of western Britain took him to Ireland, where again he landed and made observations about the people who lived there, with particular reference to the leather hide boats that were in use around that coast.

Pytheas maintained a detailed log and it is apparent that he made frequent landings during his voyage. He experienced the culture and way of life of many of the societies he visited. Although he found Britain to be a cold land he formed a good opinion of the native Britons whom he describes as being 'tall and bandy legged with white puffy skin – a people of simple habits without scheming and trickery of modern man'. (By 'modern man' he presumably means his fellow countrymen of the Mediterranean areas.)

He describes the people he met as living in log and wattle houses with stalls for cattle and within forest enclosures and forts, and the climate as 'rainy rather than snowy. In the open air the mist holds on for long so that in the course of a day the sun will only be visible for a few noontide hours.' For an astronomer taking regular fixes of the sun, this was a great disadvantage. His major complaint, apart from cold weather, was the fact that the Britons had plenty of milk but no knowledge of how to make cheese, which suggests that he and his crew had eaten their native, home provisions long before, and had been unsuccessful in replenishing this particular delicacy.

The detailed account that Pytheas gives us of Celtic Britain some two hundred years before the Roman invasion indicates that the Britons were sophisticated people who welcomed visitors and were at ease with travellers from far-off lands.

The original log written by Pytheas has never been seen by modern scholars, but fortunately it was seen by other Greek intellectuals and was extensively quoted by historians of that age. The account of the voyage not only provided information on the natural resources of Britain and the culture of its inhabitants, but also placed the British Isles on the map of the Classical world.

Pytheas was also able to prove by observation his hypothesis that there was no star at the North Pole. In around 300 BC the Pole Star was the closest star to the North Pole, but was only one of four stars forming a quadrant around it.

Pytheas returned safely to his home port of Massalia. His

voyage was a magnificent achievement, not only in terms of the skill of his seamanship and navigation, and his diplomatic and social skills which enabled him to learn so much about British society, but also in terms of scientific observation.

It was to be two hundred years before the next report on the British Isles, which was by Julius Caesar, when he mounted his successful military campaign against Britain. Subsequently a recorded circumnavigation of Britain was made by the Roman fleet the Classis Britannica in 83/84 AD, which would have provided support for Agricola's assault on the Caledonian tribes of northern Britain.

Celtic navigation

The cloudy skies and sea mists were conditions that the Celtic navigators of Britain and Gaul had to live with, and so they resorted to navigational techniques more suited to their seas than those of the Mediterranean navigators. They built up knowledge of the composition of the sea bed, recording where they would find a bottom covered in mud, fine sand, coarse gravel or shells, and would test for this using lead sounding weights tipped with tallow, so that samples could be picked up to assist in establishing a location. They also studied the formation of clouds that would develop over topographic features such as distant mountain ranges or steep-sided islands – for example the Isle of Man in the Irish Sea.

Celtic mariners also had strong tides to contend with, but because they understood the rhythmic timing of the rise and fall and the directions of tidal streams they could use these features to their advantage when planning their passage.

The Celtic mariners also placed their trust in the activities of birds, particularly migratory flocks of swans and geese. The Irish monks who voyaged so successfully to the north knew that they could set their course by following the direction of flight taken in spring and autumn by Brent Geese and Mute Swans in their annual migrations between the estuaries of the Shannon and other great Irish rivers, to Iceland, Norway and Greenland.

Tides and tidal streams

The Tides

Any visitor to Britain's coastline will see after a few hours that the level of the sea relative to the land changes in a progressive, rhythmic pattern. There are times when the sea level is high, referred to as 'high tide', when the greatest amount of beach or shore is covered, and 'low tide', when the sea retreats, exposing a wide expanse of beach or rocky foreshore. The tide is a vertical movement of sea level which occurs twice in just over 24 hours around the shores of Britain and northwest Europe. During this cycle there are two high waters and two low waters and so there are six hours when the tide advances from low to high and, having stood for a short while, there is then a six-hour period when the tide retreats to a low tide position. The time between each of the two high tides (and each of the two low tides) is around 12 hours 25 minutes, and so the times of the tides advance slightly over each period of 24 hours. This interval of time reflects the earth's rotation and the moon's revolution around the earth.

There is also another variation in tidal effects arising from the rhythmic pattern of the tidal range – the difference in height between low tide and high tide during any one period. The maximum tidal range is called a spring tide, which occurs when the high water is higher and low water lower than at any other time. For example, at Holyhead, northern Wales on Sunday the 10th September, 2006, there was a particularly high tide (a spring tide) of 5.8 metres, and a low tide of 0.4 metres, giving a tidal range of 5.4 metres, but seven days later on Sunday, 17th September, it was a neap tide, when the high tide reached only 4.4 metres and low tide fell to 2.3 metres – a tidal range of only 2.1 metres.

The rhythm of the tides and the variation in tidal ranges

is caused by the gravitational effect of the moon and also the gravitational effect of the sun, although the moon is the greater influence. The effect of the moon's gravity upon the earth is not uniform, and the surface nearer the moon experiences the greater gravitational pull, resulting in the surface of the oceans at the point nearest to the moon being pulled towards it at a faster rate than the solid earth itself, causing the water to bulge outwards and forming a high tide. At the same time a high tide is formed on the other side of the earth where the moon's gravitational effect is weaker, and the water in the ocean gets left behind as the earth experiences the stronger pull towards the moon – causing the water to bulge out that side also. In the regions between these two high tides are low tides.

When the sun and the moon are both in line with the earth the gravitational effects combine to produce a greater pull and cause the maximum tidal range – the spring tide – but when the sun and moon are at right angles to each other relative to the earth, their gravitational forces act in opposition, reducing the effect on the earth and producing neap tides.

A particularly significant feature that would have been known by the early navigators is that spring tides occur shortly after the new and full moons and neap tides occur after the quarter moon. This knowledge would have assisted them in the planning of their passage and mooring arrangements. There would be occasions when a ship's master might decide to take a short cut by using a high water spring tide to sail over areas which would be too shallow for the vessel during neap tide periods, when a long detour in deeper water would have to be made. The master of a vessel which dries out for unloading as the tide falls would also ensure that he did not dry out at the top of a spring tide, for his ship could then be stranded, perhaps for two weeks or more if the next high tide was not high enough to re-float. Knowing when spring tides were occurring would be important to early middle ages ship-masters, who would not have many deep water ports to moor in.

Another factor the mariner would have taken into account is the ability of a rising tide, particularly a spring tide, to actually stem and then reverse the flow of even major rivers along their lower, tidal reaches. As this happens the river level rises, and the flood tide would have allowed heavily laden vessels to penetrate far inland to reach trading centres for disembarking or loading cargo and passengers. During a lunar month there are two spring tides and two neap tides, and each has advantages that can be used by mariners.

When the sun is over the equator – twice a year – and also in line with the moon, even greater gravitational effects are experienced, resulting in particularly high spring tides – the Equinoctial Spring Tide – occurring around the 21st of March and the 23rd of September (the vernal and autumnal equinoxes).

Tidal streams

Tides are vertical movements of water, but their occurrence also entails mass horizontal movements of water in response to the gravitational mechanisms of the sun and moon. These horizontal movements are known as tidal streams, and an understanding of these streams was of extreme importance to early mariners reliant solely on wind or oar power to make way. An early medieval ship would be unlikely to exceed a speed of around 4 or 5 knots (4 or 5 nautical miles per hour) but the speed of a tidal stream can reach beyond this where certain features such as headlands or narrow channels affect the free flow of water. Early ships reliant solely on sail or oars would not be able to make any appreciable headway against tidal streams of the Irish Sea or Bristol Channel or the headlands of Lands End or Brittany. Mariners would therefore plan their voyages to sail with the tidal streams wherever possible, and be prepared to anchor and wait for six hours or so when the tide turned against them. In modern times navigators are able to consult tidal atlases or pilot books which clearly show the direction and strength of tidal streams on an hourly basis, and the early middle age mariners would also have compiled some rudimentary store of knowledge of the tidal characteristics of the areas through which they voyaged.

Around the coast of the British Isles and France there are numerous 'tidal gates' which are areas where the rate of the tidal stream is so strong that passage of a small vessel can only be made at specific times, or when the flow is in a particular direction. Examples of tidal gates which the voyaging saints would have had to contend with are Land's End and the Lizard of southwest England; the Sound of Mull; Strangford Lough and Carnsore Point of Ireland; the North Channel of the Irish Sea; Bardsey Sound; the Menai Strait and Carmel Head, off north-western Anglesey, in Wales.

A glance at the tidal stream charts for the Irish Sea at times of ebb and flood show how the voyaging Celtic saint's appreciation of these natural features would have assisted them in reaching their destinations along the western sea routes.

Celtic voyagers' sustenance and comfort

As long voyages were undertaken, it was also necessary to provide for the welfare and protection of the crew and passengers. Food and drink sufficient for the voyage was essential. Water could be carried in hide flasks but was subject to turning brackish in a short time, and so was not ideal for long voyages. Fortunately, the Brythons made vast quantities of beer, and cultivated orchards to provide apples for cider making. Wine was imported in bulk from Spain, Italy and Gaul and stored in pottery amphorae. These alcohol-fortified drinks provided a more stable liquid and provided a major part of the boat's provisions. Food also had to be preserved, and archaeological evidence shows that the Brythons boiled brine to extract salt, which was used to preserve surplus foods for times of scarcity. Salted lamb, beef, pork and fish would be stored on board, wrapped in leather, for consumption when required. Dried fruit and berries also formed part of the mariner's diet.

Some of the larger Romano-Celtic trading ships operating in the seas around the British Isles could provide the luxury of a cabin on deck with a cooking stove for the benefit of the crew and any passengers, but it is most unlikely that the ship's master would allow coals to be lit whilst the vessel was underway. The ship discussed earlier, which caught fire and burned down to the waterline before sinking in the harbour of St Peters Port, perhaps did so as a result of a cooking fire spreading out of control.

The Romano-Celtic vessels were not always decked, and the smaller ships, particularly the curraghs, were open to the elements, with perhaps only a small leather sheet drawn over the bow or stern to provide some shelter from rain and breaking waves. The inhospitable sea and weather of British waters made it essential for seafarers to wear protective clothing if hypothermia was to be avoided. Woollen leggings were worn under a jerkin or coat of leather treated with lanolin, which would provide waterproof protection. *The Life of St Pedrog* refers to him wearing a sheepskin coat when he voyaged to India, although he left it on a beach to be guarded by a wolf while he voyaged to an offshore island, later recovering it for his return to the colder climes of Brittany and Cornwall.

A variety of footwear was available to the voyaging saints, but to contend with the copious amount of water that would constantly inundate their feet, the most appropriate practice would be to go barefoot, or use open sandals of flax or leather which would easily drain.

The maritime infrastructure exploited by the voyaging Celtic saints was a time-served and sophisticated one, providing them with reliable and safe passage in an environment which could at times be treacherous and dangerous.

It is clear that the Celtic navigators, among them some of

the Celtic saints, had a strong knowledge of weather, geographical factors and tidal patterns. There is evidence of an efficient and organised maritime infrastructure that provided traders, ships, sailors and navigators. Armed with this knowledge, and embarking in these Celtic vessels, the saints set out on their perilous journeys, which are explored and described in the following chapters.

Chapter 5

Saints of the Old North and South Wales Provinces

More common was blood on the field's face
than ploughing of farrow

The Hall of Cynddylan, dark is the roof
Since the Saxon cut down
Powys's Cynddylan and Elfan.

The despair of Princess Heledd of Powys after a Saxon Raid

Saints of the Old North Province

St Kentigern (died 612)

Voyages: The Clyde – Carlisle – River Esk – Whithorn – Whitehaven – Llanelwy – Rhos-on-Sea – Menai Straits – Porth-clais – Llanelwy – Glasgow

The cultural links between Wales and the Old North are shown by the movements of prominent men, such as St Kentigern, a contemporary of Columba (521-597 – see chapter 6), who travelled between Strathclyde and Wales in response to political developments which made his position sometimes untenable. Men of his stature had great influence and often instigated large population movements. The movements between Wales and Strathclyde were safer and more conveniently made along the western sea routes, but the story of Kentigern has him in a miraculous voyage even before he was born. His mother was Thaneu, a step daughter of the king of the north British Kingdom of Leudaria who found herself in the unfortunate situation of being pregnant and unmarried – an entirely unacceptable state for someone in her situation – and she was sentenced to be stoned to death. Her appointed executioners, for some reason, disobeyed their orders, and decided instead to end her life by pushing her over a steep cliff in a chariot. She survived, and a holy spring gushed up from the ruts made in the ground by the chariot wheels. Thaneu's ordeal was not yet over, for she was then taken to the coast at Aberdessic and placed in a coracle with no oars or food. She was cast adrift but was fortunate to survive once more, and was washed up on a distant shore where she gave birth to Kentigern next to a fire that had been lit by shepherds.

The mother and baby were later discovered by St Serf, who adopted them both and brought up Kentigern at his church, where Kentigern received a first-class education. Kentigern was an exceptional and favoured pupil, which resulted in jealousy among other students, who turned against him, causing him to leave. In his wanderings he came across the cell of a dying monk, Fergus, whom he nursed and for whom he carried out a last wish to be buried on consecrated ground in Glasgow. Kentigern then took over the religious duties of Fergus, and at the age of twenty-five was appointed Bishop to the King of Strathclyde.

A resurgence of paganism which fostered civil war forced Kentigern to leave Strathclyde and he voyaged to the north of Wales, where there were links with the Cunedda family, and then on to southern Wales at the invitation of St David. On later returning to northern Wales, Kentigern deduced from seeing a wild boar digging a hole on the bank of the river Elwy, near Abergele, that he should found a monastery there. His foundation of the monastery is supported by a document of 1256, which records that Kentigern had built his monastery on land given to him by Malgunus of Deganwy to settle a dispute. The royal court of Deganwy was that of Cunedda's family, and this again reflects the relationship between Celtic saints and the patronage of ruling families. In this case it also indicates the common affinity of both parties with the cultural province that embraced north Wales and the lands of the Old North.

In the meantime, events in Strathclyde had proceeded from bad to worse, as the pagan princes Gwenddoleu and Morcant had raised an army, which they portrayed as representing the true Brythons (the pre-Roman, Celtic inhabitants of the area). This was to challenge Rhydderch Hael and Urien, who were accused of representing only those who had descended from the Roman colonists and the former Legionaries who had defended Hadrian's Wall, but who had remained to settle in the area when the military organization left. The two sides were divided on ethnic and religious lines, Rhydderch Hael allegedly representing Romano-British Christian interests, and Gwenddoleu British Celtic pagan beliefs. The two armies met at the battle of Arderydd on the west bank of the Esk to the north of Carlisle.

The army of Rhydderch Hael won the day. He went on to become the much-respected king of the Old North, and was eventually laid to rest on consecrated ground in northern Wales, alongside the western sea routes, where homage was paid by Manx sailors as late as the eighteenth century.

In the aftermath of the Battle of Arderydd, Rhydderch Hael summoned Kentigern back to Strathclyde to help him banish paganism and re-establish Christianity throughout the kingdom. By this time Kentigern's monastery at Llanelwy (St Asaph) was thriving, and had attracted 965 monks. Kentigern returned to Strathclyde with 665 monks and clerics, and worked with Rhydderch Hael in an energetic and far-reaching missionary campaign. Pagan shrines and images were destroyed, and even tattooing was forbidden, for this was believed to have pagan significance. Kentigern's campaign reached into the stronghold of the Picts to the north, to the Orkneys and to Norway. He visited Iona to meet Columba. St Kentigern's activities in the Old North brought followers in Glasgow, Lothian, southeast Scotland, the Forth, the Clyde, north and east Cumberland, and east Scotland.

Kentigern played a significant part in protecting Rhydderch's wife Langueth from execution as a punishment for an unwise association with a member of the Royal court. Rhydderch had given a gold ring to Langueth, but suspected his wife of taking a lover to whom she had then given the ring. When the man was sleeping Rhydderch took the ring from his finger and threw it into the Clyde. He challenged Langueth over her infidelity and asked her to produce the ring or face execution. Langueth confessed her problem to Kentigern who, after praying for her, was told that the ring was in the belly of a salmon swimming in the river. The fish was caught and the ring returned to the queen, which saved her from death. The legend is embodied in the symbol of Kentigern, which is a salmon with a ring in its mouth. It is displayed in the court of arms of the City of Glasgow and other organizations associated with Kentigern, such as the hospice charity set up in his name.

Kentigern's monastery at St Asaph in northern Wales was later named after the monk who was appointed by Kentigern to maintain it when he returned to the north. Asaph was also related to a noble family and was the grandson of the exiled north British King Pabo Post Prydion, as was St Tysilio. As a young boy Asaph received his education at Kentigern's College of Elwy and proved to be a very adept pupil who proceeded to become a monk. On one occasion Kentigern had almost passed away from hypothermia after he had stood naked in the river to say his prayers, and he called to Asaph to fetch burning coals to revive him. Asaph collected the burning coals in his monk's cowl and after taking them to Kentigern, who recovered, it was found that neither Asaph's hands nor his cowl had been burned or even scorched. He was clearly a fit person to be granted charge of such an important monastery, which still had three hundred monks even after Kentigern's departure:

St Tysilio (died 640)

Voyages: Meifod – Llandrillo-yn-Rhos – Church Island; Menai Bridge – Llantysilio – Brittany

St Tysilio's voyaging took him from the Kingdom of Powys in north-eastern Wales to Dumnonia (south-western England), and ultimately to Armorica (Brittany).

Tysilio was a nobleman, the younger son of Brochfael, King of Powys, one of the most powerful rulers of an area covering a substantial part along the eastern border of what is now central and northern Wales. Brochfael ruled from several courts throughout the kingdom, the most important of which was Pengwern Powys, alongside the river Severn at Shrewsbury. Other courts were held further north, near Welshpool; at Mathrafal, near Meifod close to where the river Fyrnwy (a tributary of the Severn) converges with the river Banwy; and at Dinas Brân, close to Llangollen in the Dee valley. The ruling Powys family was Christian and supported many churches in the Severn valley.

A bardic poem salutes Tysilio as being 'Tysilio fierce in warfare', and it is likely that he had a warrior training and upbringing as befitted a king's son in the sixth century. However, Tysilio rejected this way of life and chose a religious path, receiving instruction at Meirionnydd's principal church, Meifod, founded by Gwyddfarch under the protection of the Royal Court.

Although a monk, Tysilio retained ownership of substantial areas of land in northern Wales, particularly along the Menai Strait, the sea channel which divides Ynys Môn (Anglesey) from the mainland. This area already had a strong Christian foundation and Tysilio left Meifod to settle there, founding a church on what is now known as Ynys Tysilio (Church Island), which lies in 'the Swellies', the stretch of water in the central part of the Menai Strait.

From Meifod to Menai

Tysilio would have made passages along the coast and

estuaries of western and northern Wales in relatively small open boats, most likely coracles or curraghs, which would be ideal for the nature of his voyages. His early journeys from Meifod would have been overland to gain the upper reaches of the river Dee, which could then be navigated down to its estuary in the Irish Sea at Chester. In parts the river would have been shallow where it flowed over shoals of gravel, and the boat would have had to be hauled to deeper water. Rowing would also be necessary where the thick forests lining both banks would prevent the wind from reaching the sails. For the coastal passage along the north Wales coast to the Menai Strait, Tysilio would have transferred to a larger craft than that used on the river, but it is still likely to have been a curragh.

The northern Wales coast is strongly tidal and exposed to the prevailing west and northwesterly winds. There are few ports of refuge and the mariners would need a boat that could be quickly hauled up on to a beach should conditions deteriorate. The option of riding out a storm at sea off a lee shore would not have been a viable one. The rivers such as the Clwyd and Conwy, flowing into the Irish Sea from the Welsh mountains are extremely vigorous, and on an ebb tide produce fast currents which pose a problem even to modern vessels with powerful engines. In Tysilio's day the mariners could not even attempt an entry to these natural harbours on an ebb tide, thereby ruling them out for almost twelve hours out of twenty-four. The ability to draw up a light-weight boat onto the beach would therefore be essential. Along this part of the coast, the incoming flood tide runs strongly eastwards and the outgoing ebb runs equally strongly to the west. Good progress can be made while running with the tide, but it would be very difficult for a small boat to make any progress against an adverse tide, so it would therefore be necessary to anchor or haul out on a beach until conditions were favourable.

Tides are particularly fierce around prominent headlands, and along this stretch of the coast the massive limestone cliffs of the Great Orme, which projects five miles out into the sea, dividing Conwy Bay from Colwyn Bay, would have to be negotiated. The tide race off the Orme, particularly when the wind and tidal flow are opposed, can cause very rough-breaking seas, requiring a passage some way off shore to find calmer waters. Fortunately for Tysilio and other travellers of his era the Orme had been a destination on the western sea routes for thousands of years, because of the extensive copper mines, which had been worked throughout the Bronze Age. The waters around the headland were well-known, and on shore there would have been several timber hards (flat timber platforms laid on a shore for ships to rest on at low tide), jetties and mooring posts for the convenience of vessels awaiting loading or waiting for a suitable tide. Well-established pathways would have been constructed across the narrow, low-lying isthmus connecting the Great Orme to the main part of the coast, to enable lightweight vessels to be easily hauled overland, thereby avoiding negotiation of the dangerous headland by sea.

An alternative route may also have existed at that time, for the Afon Ganol, now just a minor culverted stream making its way into Penrhyn Bay near Llandrillo-yn-Rhos (Rhos on Sea), was once a navigable waterway that would have provided an easy bypass of the Great Orme by giving access to the river Conwy and on to Conwy Bay. In medieval times, ships were lying at anchor or pulled ashore beneath the church of Llandrillo-yn-Rhos, overlooking the valley of the Ganol, and this harbour – also held to be the departure point of Prince Madog on his voyage to North America – was in use during the early middle ages. On the promenade, which was once the beach near the location of the old harbour, is the small stone church of St Trillo, now forming part of the parish of Llandrillo-yn-Rhos.

Tysilio's continuation of his journey to the land he held on the Menai Strait took him further westwards, beneath the towering peaks of Conwy Mountain and Penmaenmawr, which form precipitous cliffs as they reach the sea and make a land passage impossible along this part of the coast. Eventually the vessel would pass the northern entrance to the sheltered Menai Strait, marked by the headland of Trwyn Du, where ancient weapons and even fish hooks dated at five thousand years of age have been found near Afon Ffraw.

Just off Trwyn Du, at the northeast shore of Ynys Môn where a lighthouse now stands, is Puffin Island (Ynys Seiriol), which supported the monastic cell forming part of the estate of the monastery of St Seiriol at Penmon, on the site of a former druid temple. The short passage from Penmon to Tysilio's church on Church Island would have been by boat through sheltered waters, with only the strong tides of the Strait having to be negotiated.

There was little Christian work for Tysilio to do in that area of Wales, for it had been under a Christian influence for at least two generations of saints, represented by such illustrious men as Seiriol, Cybi and Deiniol. This intensity of Christian worship is indicated by Ynys Môn having sixty-seven churches or chapels dedicated to saints.

Ynys Môn

On Church Island Tysilio was only a very short distance from the shore of Ynys Môn, which had been the last stronghold of the druids in Britain. The island remained pagan until Constantine proclaimed Christianity the official religion of the Roman Empire in 313.

Ynys Môn had valuable resources, particularly the production of grain, and of lead and copper, and after the Roman withdrawal from Wales it attracted the attention of the Irish tribes, particularly the Fenni, who invaded and settled along the north Wales coastal lands in large numbers. The arrival of Cunedda Wledig, Prince of Llŷn (516-542) resulted in the Irish tribes being driven out, and a period of relative stability ensued until the Saxon invasions from the east.

In the post-Roman period Ynys Môn received support of the Romano-Christian faith from Ireland and the continent, particularly Brittany, as is indicated by inscribed standing stones. Celtic Christianity developed, and the island became an area of importance, no doubt assisted by its location as a trading centre on the western sea routes. As well as Tysilio's presence, the island fostered the activities of Saints Seiriol, Cybi and Cadfan, who were contemporaries of Deiniol, the saint who established the monastery across the Menai Strait at Bangor, and was consecrated as bishop there by Prince Maelgwn of Gwynedd. Bangor had been developed as a significant settlement on one of the Roman Empire's main trade routes, and so its development as a significant religious centre was almost inevitable.

In establishing his first cell on the small island in the Menai Strait, Tysilio was able to distance himself from the aggression and warrior activities of his father and elder brother at the Royal Court of Powys, but he did not intend to adopt a hermit-like existence. Church Island is quite small, having only enough room for a small church and graveyard. It would not have supported a settlement of any great size or significance. It may well have provided a place of solitude for religious contemplation from time to time, but Tysilio possessed other land and founded a number of churches elsewhere. He encouraged others to join him and as a member of a wealthy and powerful family had no difficulty in attracting and supporting like-minded converts to his faith.

As there were many religious settlements in the Menai Strait area, further missionary work there would have been superfluous. Realising this, Tysilio concentrated his efforts in reaching out to the people in more distant areas, particularly further south along the coast, estuaries and rivers of Cardigan Bay and Pembrokeshire. His endeavours took him along the well-travelled western sea route. From Church Island in the Menai Strait, Tysilio and his travelling companions could time their passage to leave the potentially treacherous Swellies at slack water and then take the ebbing tide southwards, passing Port Dinorwic, which was later used as a safe haven by Viking raiders in the eighth century, to Caernarfon, previously the substantial Roman port of Segontium.

Tysilio initially used his church on his small island in the Menai Strait as a retreat for religious contemplation, and as a base to return to after his expeditions to broaden the influence of the Celtic Church by missionary work along the coasts and estuaries of west Wales. As a member of a wealthy and powerful family Tysilio had the financial and political resources to found and support churches, and provide training for other monks attracted to his cell.

There are a number of churches dedicated to Tysilio over a wide area stretching from his first cell at Meifod, along the Menai Strait and further south to Llandysiliogogogoch in south-western Cardiganshire and Llandysilio in Pembrokeshire. These are typical locations visited by a saint travelling the western sea routes.

On the death of King Brochfael, and whilst Tysilio was in monastic orders, his elder brother Cynan succeeded to the throne of Powys, and he in turn was succeeded by his son Selyf (Tysilio's nephew), who was defeated by the Saxon army of Aethelfrith at the battle of Chester.

St Tysilio had not chosen a military life but was still a prominent member of the royal family of Powys. He came under unwelcome pressure from Princess Hearted, the widow of one of his brothers who had been killed in the Saxon wars, to give up his holy vows and marry her, to return to the active political and military life of the royal court. This was not a choice he wished to make, and this development, together with the dangerous and uncertain circumstances in north Wales caused by Saxon invasions, may well have been the final factor that caused him to leave his small island, never to return. Not wishing to risk the possibility of bringing loss and suffering to his church and his supporters, Tysilio left the Menai Strait and voyaged down the west coast to seek refuge in communities he had founded during his missionary work. Before leaving the

Menai Strait, Tysilio and his crew had the opportunity to stop at Caernarfon to purchase and stow provisions for their voyage, while waiting for the next favourable tide to allow passage across the dangerous Caernarfon bar, upon which many vessels have been wrecked in recent and distant times. It is likely that he was still voyaging in a strong but lightly constructed hide curragh, enabling him to make coastal passages, and also negotiate the dangerous shallow bars at river mouths and navigate upstream into the estuary and hinterland beyond.

Over to Llŷn

On leaving the shelter of the Menai Strait Tysilio and his fellow voyagers faced the decision of how far to proceed by sea before disembarking and making an overland trans-peninsula trek to the waters of Cardigan Bay lying to the south. The alternative strategy of remaining at sea would require a potentially long and hazardous passage around the most westerly point of the potentially dangerous Llŷn peninsula. They would have to voyage against unfavourable prevailing winds along a rugged, inhospitable coastline subject to strong tide races and overfalls, such as those over the shoals known as the Tripods near Bardsey Island. They could face strong westerly winds and mountainous waves rolling in from an Atlantic storm, either of which could force them on to a treacherous coastline with few ports of refuge.

To avoid these perilous sea passages, the voyagers would disembark to travel overland on one of the trans-peninsula routes. They could have disembarked at one of the few sheltered havens on the north shore of the Llŷn Peninsula, such as Porth Dinllaen or Nefyn for the twenty-mile trek to the established trading port of Pwllheli, which would not only be safer but also save a sea journey of sixty miles.

Into Cardigan Bay

As Tysilio's voyage south continued, he entered Cardigan

Bay, with its graceful sweeping arc of coastline stretching from Bardsey Island to St David's Head in the south. It is a dangerous coast in strong on-shore winds, and a small boat would find itself on a very exposed lee shore set to the prevailing westerly winds. Many of the estuaries offering safe haven are impeded by bars of hard sand or gravel brought down from the mountains of Snowdonia by the rivers, which then deposit their sediment as their rate of flow falls away on meeting the sea. River bars are always highly dangerous to vessels making an entry at low water or during strong winds. As a result the mariner has only a limited access to a safe haven during unsettled weather. Some ports, such as Pwllheli or Fishguard, can offer good protection under all conditions and state of tide, but there are times when the unlucky vessel will have to ride out a storm at a sheltered anchorage such as St Tudwal's Roads (to the east of St Tudwal's Islands off Abersoch), or New Quay (towards the southern part of the bay).

As well as the hazards presented by the weather and strong tide races around the headlands, Cardigan Bay also has other dangers to trap the unwary seafarer wishing to make a coastal passage. In the northern part of the Bay there are three dangerous shoals extending some considerable distance seawards from the shore. The longest and most dangerous of these is St Patrick's Causeway (Sarn Badrig), a shoal of loose rocks and stones reaching about twelve miles out into the bay near Harlech. There are no clues as to why St Patrick's name should be associated with this natural structure, other than it perhaps being assumed by local inhabitants that it was so long that it once reached out to Ireland, enabling the saint to visit Wales without getting his feet wet. The other two shoals are to the south: Sarn y Bwch near Tywyn reaches over six miles seawards from the estuary of Afon Dysynni, and the Sarn Gynfelyn, lying a few miles north of Aberystwyth harbour, although shorter, are still four miles in length and a navigation hazard under certain conditions.

These two shoals, like Sarn Badrig, are composed of large loose stones and gravel patches, probably remnants of moraines left by the retreating Irish Sea ice-sheet during the last Glacial period. A more romantic tradition is that the shoals are the remains of the dykes that protected the ancient land of Cantre'r Gwaelod, which was flooded and lost when a night-watchman failed to close the sluice gates against the incoming tide. The remains of a submerged forest are exposed at low tides and dating of the tree stumps indicate an age of around five thousand years, so there is certainly a basis for some folk memory of extensive lands which became inundated when sea levels rose after the last Ice Age.

At the north-eastern corner of Cardigan Bay is Tremadog Bay, which receives the waters of the Afon Glaslyn, and which for centuries has been a safe haven for mariners and offered a landing point for Celtic saints making use of the estuary to reach inland along the river banks.

Tysilio would have sailed into all of the river estuaries accessible to his small boat, for it is along the lower reaches of river valleys that the most fertile agricultural land and consequently the largest settlements were to be found. Navigation from the sea would not be a problem for an experienced mariner because of the many natural topographic features of this coastline. Pwllheli is clearly marked by Gimblet Rock, a 40-foot (12 metre) high conspicuous mass of granite south of the harbour entrance. Also along this stretch of coastline, the majestic backdrop provided by the mountains of Snowdonia provides distinctive waypoints of reference. Barmouth, situated on the well-defined Mawddach estuary, while being impossible to enter in strong on-shore winds, is easily identified by noting the 2,930ft/893m peak of Cader Idris (Pen y Gadair) to the southeast and a small rounded hill on the south side of the harbour. Once the estuary has been entered the river is navigable for ten miles or so upstream.

Some of these settlements, such as Porthmadog on the Glaslyn estuary, may have been Christian as a result of the

Roman influence emanating from the nearby Roman fort and Roman road, which would have given access to cosmopolitan traders and settlers as well as Legionaries. On withdrawal of the Roman presence it is likely that the deeply-rooted pagan practices of the region would have re-emerged until the arrival of the Irish and Breton missionaries of the fifth century.

The story of St Tydecho, a brother of St Samson, indicates the richness of agricultural land near estuaries. Tydecho had a cell on the bank of the Mawddach estuary, where he wore a horsehair shirt and slept on a bare slate bed. He was tormented by Maelgwn Gwynedd who scattered Tydecho's horses in mid winter, expecting them to starve, but Tydecho protected them by prayer so that they returned in spring better fed than before. Maelgwn then stole his oxen, but Tydecho was visited by deer who pulled his plough for him. Then Maelgwn came to taunt Tydecho and sat on his slate bed, but became stuck to it and could not move. He begged to be released, apologised to Tydecho, and returned his oxen, after which Tydecho lived an undisturbed holy existence.

Aberdyfi, further south along the coast, was also a haven for voyaging saints. From the sea it was the first major inlet south of Cader Idris, with steep hills on the north side of its estuary and lower ground to the south. Both Barmouth and Aberdyfi would be typical of the localities sought by monks such as Tysilio, travelling by sea to reach populations and settlements to which Christianity could be introduced.

While it is not possible to positively identify Tysilio with all of the Cardigan Bay locations, the founding of a church at Llandysilio in Pembrokeshire, mid-way along the overland route from Cardigan Bay to Milford Haven on the south coast of Wales, is positive evidence of his activities in that area. He is likely to have left his ship at a port on the river Teifi, perhaps in the region of modern-day Cardigan or St Dogmael's (commemorating another well-travelled Celtic saint) and trekked overland to reach the upper reaches of the Eastern Cleddau river, from where he would voyage downstream to Milford Haven to continue his journey by sea.

In reaching this area of southern Wales Tysilio had moved out of the influence of the north Wales saints and entered the localities more attuned to the southern Wales cults under the influence of St David, Illtud, Teilo, Cadog and Dyfrig. He was now within easy reach of the great monastic centre of Llanilltud Fawr, founded by Illtud, and he would no doubt have extended his travels to receive instruction and exchange views with his fellow Christians. Here he would also have the opportunity to learn of the latest news and contacts at Celtic Christian religious settlements in Cornwall and Brittany.

The invasion of Powys by Aethelfrith's Saxons, their slaughter of the monks at Bangor Is-coed, and their further attacks on Ynys Môn gave Tysilio and many others little alternative but to seek safe refuge elsewhere. At this time it would be natural for him to return to the communities and religious centres he had visited or founded during his missionary activities. He may have decided after a period of further discussion and reflection that his future lay in the religious life of Brittany, where there was a strong Celtic community which still required missionary work amongst its Frankish neighbours. This would be attractive to a man of Tysilio's background and so he departed, never to return to his northern Wales homeland.

St Elen (died early fifth century)

Elen Luyddoc, also known as St Helen, was the daughter of King Eudaf who ruled Ewyas, part of west Herefordshire, and was the wife of the Roman governor Magnus Maximus, who was elected Emperor by his soldiers. When Maximus arrived in Wales he apparently had a dream about a beautiful Welsh princess called Helen. After following the directions given in his dream Maximus found Helen at Caernarfon, where he married her and gave her the fortifications of Caernarfon, Caerleon and Carmarthen as a wedding gift. It was from Segontium – the Roman military base at Caernarfon – that Magnus Maximus (also known by his Welsh name Macsen Wledig) withdrew the last of the Roman troops from Wales in 383 AD, but that was not the last of the associations of his family with the area. On leaving Wales Maximus and his family established the Imperial Court at Treves in France where he and Helen were patrons of Martin of Tours. Maximus was killed in 388 and Helen returned to Wales, where she was venerated as St Elen. Churches are dedicated to her in various parts of northern and southern Wales such as Capel Elen on Ynys Môn and Llanelen in the Gower and in Gwent. She was also the mother of saints, the most famous being Cystennin ap Maxen Wledig, with dedications at Llangystennin in Caernarfonshire, Llangwstennin in the valley of the Afon Ganol, near Llandrillo-yn-Rhos, Conwy and elsewhere.

St Dwynwen (died 465)

At the southeast end of the Menai Strait on the Ynys Môn side is Llandwyn Island, an important navigational mark for mariners entering or leaving the Strait and in modern times the site of a lighthouse, pilot station and lifeboat station. Llandwyn Island, which is accessible today at low tide, is named after St Dwynwen who died there in 465. She is commemorated as the Welsh patron saint of lovers, although she did not appear to have had fulfilment in that aspect of her life, for legend tells that while she found happiness in a young man by the name of Maelon, her father, King Brychan, did not approve and ordered her to cease her relationship with him. For good measure Dwynwen was also given a potion by God which quenched her passion and turned Maelon into a block of ice. Her island became a place of pilgrimage, and a festival in her name is celebrated annually on the 25th of January.

St Seiriol (sixth century)

Voyages: Penmon, Ynys Môn – Rome – Penmon

Seiriol is associated with the abbey of Penmon, which lies on the Menai Strait at the northeast tip of Ynys Môn and which was founded by his brother, King Einion (St Einion), grandson of Cunedda Wledig, Prince of Llŷn (516-542). As an extension to this settlement a cell and chapel was constructed on Puffin Island, which lies just off shore from the main island. It is not possible to land on Puffin Island as it is now a bird sanctuary, but the tall stone tower of a ruined monastic building there is a conspicuous landmark. Penmon Abbey itself is also a prominent structure, now under the protection of CADW, and the ruins of the monk's refectory, the dove cote, the spring and St Seiriol's Church make it a worthwhile visit.

St Seiriol was a friend of St Cybi whose church at Caergybi (Holyhead) was on the west of Ynys Môn, and the two men often walked to meet each other at a half way point. This practice meant that Seiriol walked west each morning, with the sun on his back, as it was again in the afternoon when he returned to Penmon. In contrast, Cybi had the sun in his face when he walked east in the morning and west in the afternoon, therefore becoming tanned whilst Seiriol remained pale. The two saints were therefore referred to as Seiriol Wyn and Cybi Felyn, the names indicating that Seiriol was white or pale and Cybi was tanned.

St Cybi (sixth century)

Voyages: Padstow – Tenby – Llangybi – Caergybi (Holyhead)

Cybi was born in Cornwall but was associated with north Wales where he founded a church within the walls of the abandoned Roman fort on land granted to him by Maelgwn, the King of Gwynedd at Holyhead (Caergybi) on Ynys Môn. He is buried on Bardsey Island (Ynys Enlli). Like Tysilio he came from a distinguished royal family; his mother was

Gwen, the sister of Non, mother of St David. His coastal voyaging on the way to northern Wales is commemorated by dedications to him in southern Cornwall and at Llangybi in Pembrokeshire.

St Cadfan (fifth century)
Voyages: Brittany –Tywyn – Bardsey Island

When St Cadfan and his followers landed at Tywyn in 516, this stretch of coast received one of northern Wales' most influential Celtic missionaries. Cadfan, who was exiled from Brittany, was from a noble family and was a ruler as well as a priest. This status is commemorated by the Latin inscription on Carreg Cadfan, a standing stone of 625 AD at Llangadwaladr recording that he was 'the wisest of all kings'. The church at Llangadwaladr served the Royal Court at Aberffraw and commemorates Cadfan's grandson who was canonised as 'The Beatified St Cadwaladr, King and Chieftain of Britain' some twenty-five years after his death in 664 AD.

Cadfan used the western sea routes to reach Wales, where he had significant influence on the religious life of the area. He became the first abbot of Ynys Enlli, but it was at Tywyn that he built his first church, which was to become the mother church of his cult.

In the present church at Tywyn is Maen Cadfan, one of the most important ancient relics in Wales. It is an oblong stone inscribed on four sides with the oldest written example of Welsh on Welsh soil. Maen Cadfan was inscribed around 750 AD, some two hundred years after Cadfan's era, and was not a memorial to the saint but to a number of prominent people of the time. Its importance derives from the fact that the language used on the stone is early Welsh (Cymraeg Cynnar), which developed from the Old Celtic Brythonic spoken in the Old North (yr Hen Ogledd). Early Welsh remained in use until around 850. Other dedications to Cadfan in the locality between the Dysynni and the Dyfi rivers are Pistyll Cadfan (Cadfan's waterfall), Eisteddfa Cadfan (Cadfan's chair), Llwybr Cadfan (Cadfan's path), and Morfa Cadfan, a street. The old harbour is no longer visible but its former location is recorded in the name 'Gwaliau' (sea walls) on the road behind the church.

Several churches in the area of Tywyn, such as Llanfihangel on the upper reaches of the Dysynni, have circular churchyards which indicate a very ancient site, despite the later, medieval dedications such as to St Michael. The area had been an important population centre since pre-historical times, as indicated by cromlechs and standing stones, as well as the later Bronze and then Iron Age settlements of early Celtic times. There are the remains of a number of significant Celtic hill forts, the most impressive being at Craig yr Aderyn near Tywyn. During the Roman period a fort was built at Pennal to protect the economically important copper mines. It is likely that copper from here was traded along the western sea routes, a trade that developed the harbour of Tywyn and disseminated knowledge of the community that grew up around it. The river Dyfi was also a politically important area and formed the boundary of three ancient kingdoms – Powys, Gwynedd and Y Deheubarth. In the sixth century Maelgwn Gwynedd met other princes on the banks of the Dyfi at Traeth Maelgwn (Maelgwn's beach) near Ynys-las to agree their political boundaries.

Cadfan's choice of Tywyn as a base from which to develop his cult was clearly not accidental, for the area had been of major international importance for a very long period before his arrival. Mariners navigating to Wales from Brittany would have set a course to take them safely off Land's End at the south-western tip of Cornwall, and those intending to make a landing in Cardigan Bay or northern Wales would also steer to clear the southwestern peninsula of Pembrokeshire. The direction of the tidal stream flowing into the Irish Sea would then sweep them northwards to pass the Llŷn in northern Wales. The master of a ship intending to land at Tywyn, and having passed the towering granite cliffs of Pembrokeshire and the dangers of Ramsey Island, would have to make a positive change of course to leave the main northwards-flowing tidal stream, and sail on an easterly heading into Cardigan Bay. The ship's master would need to have a specific requirement to take his vessel into Cardigan Bay, otherwise he would not do so, for he would run the risk of his ship being trapped there by prevailing westerly winds blowing the vessel onto a lee shore with very few safe havens.

Cadfan did not travel alone to Cardigan Bay, for he led a group of monks who would have wide-reaching influence in the religious development of central and northern Wales. His followers included Padarn, Sulien, Trillo Baglan, Sadwrn, Mael, and others who adopted the strategy of establishing a church at their landfall and then making their way inland to spread their influence. Two other Breton monks – St Tannwg and St Eithras also established themselves in the central Cardigan Bay area near Tywyn, and are commemorated at the church at Pennal.

Cadfan became established at Tywyn before he became the abbot of the monastery on Bardsey Island. Sulien and Mael voyaged northwards along the coast to establish Cwm Church in Flintshire before moving inland along the river Dee to Corwen.

Cadfan's cousin, Tudwal, a Cornishman by birth, is also associated with northern Wales, particularly Llŷn, where he founded an abbey on St Tudwal's Island off the coast near Abersoch. He is also commemorated in Brittany, where he founded a large monastery at Treguier.

St Trillo (probably fifth century)

Voyages: Brittany – Tywyn – Llandrillo-yn-Rhos.

St Trillo was one of the group of monks who accompanied Cadfan on his voyage from Brittany to Tywyn and then continued northwards along the Welsh coast to fulfil his missionary duties. Trillo sailed first of all to Bardsey Island, then around Llŷn to negotiate the Menai Strait and eastwards along the coast, rounding the precipitous limestone cliffs of Great Orme to land at Llandrillo-yn-Rhos (Rhos-on-Sea). Here he established his small chapel on the beach after discovering a holy well where a Celtic cross of light appeared as a column. This small chapel is still open for worship at Llandrillo-yn-Rhos, and its holy well still flows. After founding this chapel Trillo continued voyaging eastwards along the northern Wales coast and then entered the tidal estuary of the river Dee, eventually leaving his boat to trek over the hills to Llandrillo-yn-Edeirnion near Corwen in Denbighshire. At his church here his holy well is said to cure rheumatism, and there are also dedications to his fellow monks, Sulien and Mael, with whom he had left Brittany in Cadfan's party.

Bardsey Island (Ynys Enlli) and St Tudwal's Islands.

Bardsey Island, lying off Llŷn, is only 1.5 miles by 0 .75 miles but is of monumental significance to the Age of Saints. It presents to the sea a rugged shore of steep cliffs, although there is a safe landing place. It is now home to a farm and nature reserve, preserving the tranquillity of this holy island. The boat trip from the mainland to the island is of no great distance, but is as hazardous now as it was in the Age of Saints. The present day farm has to endure the difficulties caused when high winds and rough seas result in suspension of ferry services to the mainland provided by a small boat. In recent times the annual transfer by boat of Bardsey's flock of sheep to market on the mainland was delayed so long by persistent bad weather that concern arose over the diminishing supply of their fodder.

The Llŷn Peninsula and its islands of Bardsey and Tudwal is one of the most important locations in the consideration of Celtic Christianity and its voyaging saints. The saints associated with the area are amongst the most influential of the Celtic Church. Whereas early Christianity in many other areas of post-Roman Britain, such as southeast Wales, was introduced and sustained by the Roman Church, this had little influence in northeast Wales, particularly Llŷn. Here Christianity was fundamentally Celtic in its form and was introduced by voyaging monks from Brittany, Cornwall and Ireland.

St Cadfan was the first Abbot of Ynys Enlli. The monastery there was founded by the benefactor King Einion (St Einion), grandson of Cunedda Wledig, Prince of Llŷn, who gave the island and the monastery to Cadfan. Einion also founded the monastery of Penmon, Ynys Môn, which he gave to his brother St Seiriol.

St Dyfrig, who is referred to by Geoffrey of Monmouth as the uncle of the legendary King Arthur and who crowned Arthur when he was fifteen, died on Ynys Enlli in 546 although his remains were removed to Llandaff in 1120. The great Celtic saint Deiniol was also buried on Ynys Enlli, which became a retreat for dying Celtic monks.

Saints of the South Wales Province

St David (520 – 589)

Voyages: Aberaeron – Porth-clais – Ireland – Cornwall – Rome – Jerusalem – Porth-clais.

St David, patron saint of Wales, is probably the most significant of the Celtic saints associated with southern Wales. The county of Ceredigion is named after one of Cunedda's sons, Ceredig, who became king of the land between the Dyfi and the Teifi after the Irish tribes had been driven out of northern Wales. St David is thought to have been the son of Sandde, one of Ceredig's descendents in the line of the kings of Ceredigion, and his mother was Non. He was born in around 520 somewhere in central Ceredigion and educated at Henfynyw, a teaching monastery to the south of Aberaeron. Although St David is the patron saint of Wales his influence was not universal through the area now delineated by the present boundaries. His cult is strongest in

SIGNIFICANT MOTHER CHURCHES IN WALES

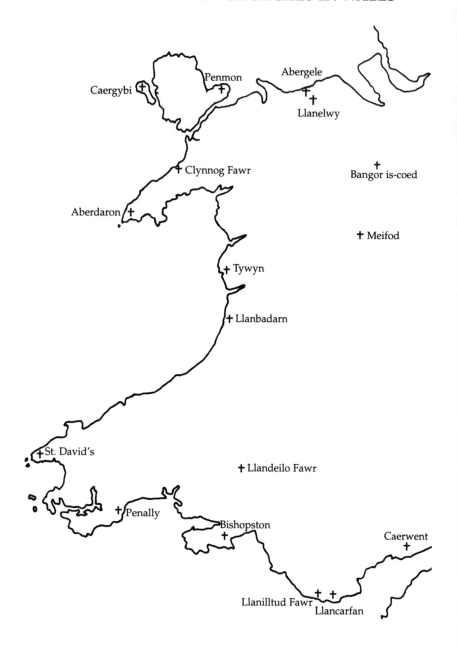

south-western Wales, where, in the Aberaeron region, there are over a dozen churches dedicated to him. There are hardly any dedications to St David in northern Wales and little evidence of St David going any further north than the Afon Wyre, near Llanrhystud, which may have been a geographical boundary between the cultural and political provinces within Wales at that time. There is evidence that St David travelled to southeast Wales and the Welsh borderlands using the old Roman roads, and also coastal routes along the shore of the Bristol Channel, resulting in dedications to him in Carmarthenshire, the Gower, the river valleys of the Tywi and Wye, in Radnorshire and Herefordshire. The church dedicated to St David (Dewi) at Henfynyw (Old Menevia) incorporates the name 'Mynyw' (Latin Minerva), which is also the old name for Tyddewi (St David's). As well as these travels through Wales and its borderlands St David also voyaged along the western sea routes to Ireland, Brittany and Cornwall where there are dedications to him.

The earliest written evidence of St David's voyages comes from a reference in the Irish Catalogue of Saints, written around 730, which tells that the Irish were given Mass by Bishop David and the Britons, Gildas and Teilo. The later Irish Martyrologies state that his monastery was located at Minevia, the present day St David's. In the fifth and sixth centuries there were strong cultural links between southeast Wales and the Waterford area of Ireland, from where the Deisi tribe, who settled in Pembrokeshire, had originated. St David's first contact with an Irish priest was at a very early age – shortly after his birth he was baptised in the water of the harbour of Porth-clais, by St Elvis, bishop of Emlech in Ireland. In later years St David sailed from this same harbour, near his monastery at Minevia, embarking in his curragh to cross the southern Irish Sea to the rivers and ports of Waterford, Wexford and Wicklow. As a result of his travels in Ireland St David is associated with several prominent Irish monks, such as Ailbe, Declan, Aidan, Finnian of Clonard and

Senan. The first three of these Irish saints are associated with religious sites on the rivers of south and southeast Ireland where the waters of the Slaney in Loch Garmon, the river Suir of Waterford and river Lee of Cork fed the stream of maritime traffic, including that of the Celtic saints along the western sea routes. St David also visited Senan at his settlement on the river Shannon, and travelled into central Ireland to meet Finnian at his monastery at Clonard.

St David's voyages in the course of his missionary duties and his own learning have been traced along the Welsh coast and rivers, across the Irish Sea and along many Irish rivers. He also undertook the long sea voyages necessary for a legendary pilgrimage to Rome and Jerusalem with his fellow monks Padarn and Teilo. All of these voyages were from his church in Pembrokeshire, where St David's Cathedral now stands, giving him immediate access to the western sea routes through the small, natural harbour of Porth-clais, located in a small drying inlet three miles west of Solva.

St Padarn (died 550)

Voyages: Brittany – Aberystwyth – Cornwall – Porth Clais – Jerusalem – southern Wales

St Padarn was a contemporary of St David, and was prominent in the Aberystwyth area where he founded the region's most important church at Llanbadarn. The town of Aberystwyth was once known as Llanbadarn Gaerog (Fortified Llanbadarn) – a name evocative of two dominant elements of early middle ages society: Celtic Christianity and unsettled times. Padarn's original church was destroyed by Danish raiders in 988 and its replacement destroyed in the turbulent period of the eleventh century. There are two other churches dedicated to Padarn in the county and also a chapel near the beach. Some legends tell of Padarn being a Breton who came to Wales with Cadfan and Tydecho, and received training under Illtud at Llanilltud Fawr. He worked extensively in north and mid Wales and has dedications in

THE VOYAGES OF WELSH SAINTS TO IRELAND AND THE NORTH BRITONS

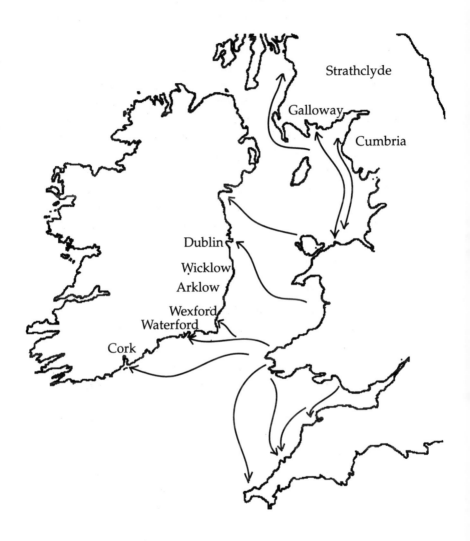

Powys, Gwynedd and Dyfed. He also travelled to Cornwall, where he has dedications, and legend tells that he accompanied St David and Teilo to Rome and Jerusalem.

Aberystwyth was also a destination for other Celtic saints such as Crannog, Deiniol and the Irish Ffraid. Other former ports along the coast of Cardigan Bay, such as Harlech, Cardigan and Aberaeron, which have suffered from the silting up of their harbours, were known to have fishing and ship-building activities in Norman and early medieval times, which is a good indication that these were accessible ports and settlements as far back as the post-Roman period. Aberarth, now a small village, is certainly one of the oldest ports in Ceredigion, and low tide reveals the remains of ancient stone fish weirs built by Cistercian monks. Aberarth was likely to have been the port at which many Celtic saints would have landed, and there are a number of churches in the area dedicated not only to Padarn but also to Tysilio, Ffraid, Crannog, and Ceitho.

St Justinian (sixth century)
Voyages: Brittany – Solva (Porth Clais) – Ramsey Island.

Most travellers voyaging around the coast of Wales would take the trans-peninsula route over Pembrokeshire, to avoid the perils of the most southwesterly part of the coastline known today as St David's Peninsula, but the ruggedness, remoteness, and the hostility of the seas in the area were natural attractions for Celtic saints seeking retreat. Such a saint was Justinian, a Breton nobleman who became a priest and, as one of a group of missionaries, made an expedition to Wales. Justinian impressed St David, who gave him buildings on Ramsey Island and the mainland. There are indications that Justinian may have been an autocratic, domineering man, which might give a clue to his untimely death. Perhaps to cloak the true circumstances, an elaborate myth was generated.

Justinian decided to create a hermitage on Ramsey Island but when he arrived there he found it already occupied by St

Honarius, who was living a devout life with his sister and her maid. Justinian said he would settle there but only if the two women were sent away. Honarius at first rejected the request but Justinian prevailed. Legend tells that the island was connected to the land by a causeway used by local people, and that Justinian became so annoyed at the passage of visitors disturbing his work that he cursed the causeway, making it disappear beneath the waves; only a collection of rocks known as 'The Bitches' remained. This was not well received by the local people, for after the disappearance of the causeway the only means of getting between Ramsey and the mainland was by boat. There was a community on the island and Justinian is known to have been a hard and uncompromising taskmaster over the workers who tended his land.

Another legend about Justinian tells that he was approached by sailors who informed him that St David was ill, and offered to take him to see him. During the voyage to the mainland Justinian realised from their ugliness that they were devils and so recited Psalm 79, turning them into black crows that flew away at the appropriate verse. On proceeding to see St David, Justinian found him to be in good health and then knew he had been tricked. The devils tried again: they entered three of Justinian's workers when he instructed them to work harder. These workers flew into a rage, attacked him and cut off his head. Justinian's headless body picked up the decapitated head and 'glided across the sea' to the mainland, where it was laid to rest and where a church was built over it. Holy springs that cured the infirm gushed forth from two places where the severed head had touched the ground. The three murderers became afflicted with leprosy and were banished to an isolated outcrop known as 'Leper's Rock'.

St Brynach (died 570)

Voyages: Ireland – Cardigan – Jerusalem – Nevern, Wales;
or:
Ireland – Cardigan – Rome – Braunton, Devon.

Brynach was a pagan Irish nobleman who converted to Christianity and then sailed to south-western Wales, landing possibly at Cardigan. He set up his cell in a former Iron Age hill fort at Carn Ingli (Hill of Angels), three miles southwest of Nevern. He married the daughter of Clutor, a local chieftain, who also granted him land along the valley of the river Gwaun, upon which Brynach founded three churches. In the Church of St Brynach, dedicated to him at Nevern, there are a number of important inscribed stones. Two of these are inside the church and now form windowsills in the south transept, but were found in 1906 embedded in the wall of a passage. One of these, known as the Maglocunus Stone, is probably of the fifth century and inscribed in both Ogham and Latin. This stone commemorates Maglocunus (Maelgwn), son of Clutor although it is not known if this is the same Clutor who gave his daughter's hand in marriage to Brynach. The other of these stones is of the tenth century and bears a Viking pattern. Outside in the churchyard there are two more inscribed stones. The Vitalianus Stone also bears bilingual inscriptions in Ogham and Latin whilst the other is a Celtic cross of the tenth century upon which the first cuckoo of spring is alleged to sing on St Brynach's Day (the 7th of April).

One legend tells us that, after his activities in Wales, Brynach became another saint who acquired the skill of travelling over the water without a boat. From Wales he made a pilgrimage to the Holy Land, where he is reputed to have killed a dragon, before sailing back to Wales on a stone. When he returned to Wales he found a degree of Irish hostility had developed and in one skirmish he was attacked and wounded by a spear. His friends took him to a holy well where his wound was washed and healed. He was forced to find a new site for his church but his first choice at Abergwaun was later found to be inhabited by evil spirits who could not be dislodged. At the next site, timber he had cut down for construction of buildings was stolen by local inhabitants, but his perseverance was rewarded by an invitation to found the church at Nevern. This legend contradicts an alternative story which tells that after Brynach had founded his churches in Wales he left for a long pilgrimage to Rome and on his return to Britain he settled at Braunton in Devon, where suckling pigs showed him where to build a church. In Devon he is referred to as St Brannoc.

St Teilo (520 – 580)

Voyages: Penally, near Tenby – Porth Clais – Ireland – Rome – Jerusalem – Llandaff, Cardiff – Cornwall – Dol, Brittany – Llanilltud Fawr – Llandeilo Fawr

Teilo was active along the river estuaries and shores of the Bristol Channel bordering south Wales and inland along the old Roman roads through Radnorshire, Breconshire and Gwent. He was born into a pagan family, probably at Penally, near Tenby in Pembrokeshire, where he founded a monastic community, although unfortunately, apart from the shrine of a saint, believed to be that of Teilo, no other traces remain there. Most of Teilo's work was centred on Llandeilo Fawr in Carmarthenshire and the churches dedicated to him indicate he travelled along the rivers Tywi and Teifi.

Teilo was also a pupil of St David, Paul Aurelian, and Dyfrig. He lived in the very unsettled political environment of western Britain. When the south Irish pagan tribes invaded Glyn Rhosyn (St David's Peninsula) of south-western Wales, he left the area and made a legendary pilgrimage to Rome and Jerusalem with St David and Padarn, eventually returning to Llandaff in southeast Wales with a holy bell that had been given to him by the Patriarch of Jerusalem, in recognition of being the best preacher. After work in Llandaff he voyaged to Cornwall, but in 547 the onset of the yellow plague epidemic that swept the country caused him to make a sudden departure to stay with Samson at Dol in Brittany, where he remained for seven years. In Brittany Teilo fought and killed a dragon and threw it into the sea. He also planted an orchard of apple trees, which reached from Dol to Cai and which was much valued for the production of cider.

Teilo returned to Wales at a time when the Angles of eastern Britain invaded Wales by crossing the old border at the river Wye. Their advance was blocked at Llandeilo Gresynni by Prince Iddon of Gwent, who called upon Teilo to provide both military and spiritual leadership to the defending Britons. Teilo surveyed the scene of the ensuing battle from a hill and then, issuing curses against the invading forces, assisted the men of Gwent in achieving a decisive victory over the Angles. For his vital leadership in this battle, which kept south Wales free of pagan invaders, Teilo was rewarded by the Prince of Gwent with a gift of the land upon which the battle was fought and the hill from which Teilo had surveyed the scene. St Teilo later died at Llandeilo Fawr in south-western Wales.

St Illtud (450 525)

Voyages: Llanilltud Fawr – Auxerre – Brittany, Poullon, near Dournanez – Briec, Cornwall – Llanilltud Fawr – Caldy Island

One of the first in a long line of highly respected Welsh saints was Dyfrig (Dubricius), who is associated with Hereford, Caerleon and the Wye valley, and who was a bishop in the Romano-British tradition. Dyfrig was resolute against the changes sweeping through Britain, and provided strong leadership to the Christian community, resisting a reversion to the pagan worship that was still prevalent in areas of the upper reaches of the Severn estuary, such as the Forest of Dean.

Illtud as one of Wales' most influential Christian leaders

succeeded Dyfrig; this succession also heralded a change in ecclesiastical philosophy from the Roman to monastic tradition that was to become a feature of the Celtic church.

At Llanilltud Fawr, Illtud took the title of Abbot, rather than Bishop. This was to indicate that his philosophy was rooted in the monastic traditions developed by Anthony in Egypt and also adapted in the French monasteries by Martin of Tours and St Honorat at Lerins – a tradition that reflected the interchange of ideas carried along the western sea routes from the Middle East and continental Europe.

Illtud was born into a royal family. He is given an illustrious heritage: his mother was one of the daughters of the King of Britain, and her sister was Arthur's mother. Illtud, who was therefore King Arthur's cousin, served as one of his knights until his conversion by St Cadog. Before becoming a monk, Illtud had received a military training, and he experienced life as a soldier and commander in military campaigns in Gaul, where he was referred to as 'one of Gaul's most eloquent children'. He received his education in the tradition of the Roman schools and was also educated and ordained by Germanus of Auxerre, possibly in Britain, when Germanus was sent there by Pope Celestinus in 429 and 435 to restore orthodox teaching.

Illtud became renowned for the monastery he founded at Llanilltud Fawr (Llantwit Major) in 500, and which continued as a seat of monastic learning until Norman times. Illtud earned great respect throughout the Celtic world and was unequalled in stature during his lifetime. Wealthy families would take their children to Llanilltud Fawr to receive the best education available anywhere in western Europe. One of the testaments to Illtud's stature appears in the Life of Samson of Dol, which was written in a monastery in Brittany:

> Llantwit was the school of the famous master of the Britons, Eltut by name and the most learned of all the Britons in his knowledge of the Scripture, the Old

Testament, the New Testament and all branches of Philosophy – poetry, rhetoric, grammar, and arithmetic – and all of the theories of philosophy. And by birth he was a wise magician, having knowledge of the future.

Illtud travelled throughout south Wales, Brittany and Cornwall, and a church on Caldy Island off the Welsh coast still bears his name. Most other churches dedicated to him are in south-eastern Wales (in Glamorgan and Breconshire); in Gower, where he formed a church at Oystermouth; and at Llanelltud in Merionnydd. His influence on the educational and ecclesiastical development of Celtic Christianity was monumental, and many of his pupils such as Gildas, Samson and St David were to continue his principles in their own work. Illtud was clearly a dynamic leader, always aware of the needs of the communities he served, as shown by his direct action in arranging a convoy of grain ships to set sail from south Wales to Brittany to relieve a famine there. He is associated in Brittany with the churches of Leon, Treguier and Vannes, which indicate his sphere of interest and veneration in those areas.

The other great teaching monastery of southeast Wales was founded by another pioneer of Christianity in Wales, St Cadog, at Llancarfan. The siting of both monasteries was favourable for receiving sea-borne travellers. Both monasteries were on the north shore of the Bristol Channel but far enough to the west to be clear of the muddy, marshy coastal regions of the Severn estuary. The monasteries were also near the old Roman road across the south Wales coastal plain, and in a previously Romanised Christian area.

Illtud's monastery at Llanilltud Fawr was also close to the Royal Court of Dinas Powys and also the site of one of the largest Roman villas in Wales. The archaeological evidence of pottery, and other household items, originating from Greece, Alexandria and France found at Dinas Powys confirm the strong maritime links with those areas. Coastal voyages around the Welsh coast were usually made in the hide curraghs or large coracles, but trading vessels like those of the grain ships voyaging to Brittany and beyond, would have been constructed of heavy planks and frames to enable them to carry a heavy or valuable cargo that would require protection from the weather during offshore passages.

In areas like the Severn estuary east of Llanilltud Fawr and Llancarfan the foreshore is low-lying and muddy and so gently inclined timber frames, known as hards, had to be constructed, upon which a flat-bottomed cargo vessel would rest after a falling tide. Remains of these hards are found in sheltered areas such as Magor and Goldcliff in southeast Wales. It is from locations such as these that Illtud's grain ships are likely to have departed for Brittany. Here the vessel and its cargo would not be damaged by the pounding of the waves as the tide receded, and timber causeways would have been constructed to give access for loading and unloading.

It is almost certain that smaller vessels, perhaps carrying only passengers or light cargoes, could have been received at Llanilltud Fawr itself, which is located in the valley of the small Ogney brook; this brook drained into the river Colhugh and gave access to the sea. A visitor today would probably consider it impossible for a sea-going vessel of any description to make its way up this river, but it was almost certainly navigable in Illtud's day – indeed the ease of access to the sea and its seaways would be a prime consideration for the establishment of a monastery. Another consideration was security, and the Llanilltud Fawr site also meets this requirement, for it is located beyond a sharp bend in the river that shields it from the view of raiders and pirates approaching from the sea.

The saints who voyaged to Cornwall

The south-western peninsula of Britain was the destination of voyagers from both Wales and Ireland, each taking with them particular aspects of their culture. The Irish influence is identified through the whole of the peninsula but is derived from different sources. In the east, impinging into Somerset, Devon and east Cornwall, there are dedications to Welsh saints as well as Ogham-inscribed stones and dedications to the 'Children of Brychan' which indicates that some Irish saints had made their way to those areas via south Wales.

In the far west, beyond Perranporth and Falmouth, the dedications are almost entirely Irish, and the remains of 'grass marked' decorated pottery comparable to Souterian ware of northeast Ireland and the Kingdom of Dalriada have been found here. The Irish saints commemorated in this area are associated with St Breuca and others from the Leinster and Ulster areas, which indicate direct voyages from Ireland, in contrast to those who had used southern Wales as an intermediate settlement and staging post. These saints had voyaged on an outward route from the Irish Sea to make landfall in the most westerly part of Cornwall.

However the group of saints who laboured most comprehensively throughout Cornwall were those who voyaged across the 'Northern Sea' (Bristol Channel) from Wales. This group of saints is associated with specific localities in both Wales and Cornwall, particularly the Padstow/Bodmin/Newquay areas, which indicates cult influences or perhaps combined missionary expeditions. Many of the group are also associated with Brittany and some also with Ireland. St Teilo, whose activities along the river Teifi have already been mentioned, is just one who is also dedicated in Cornwall and Brittany. Prominent members of the group, along with Teilo, are Cadfan, Cadog, Crannog, Briog, Decuman and Petrog.

The dangers of landing on Cornwall's northern coast

The maritime routes through the Bristol Channel and St George's Channel were absolutely essential in feeding the growth of Celtic Christianity, but their use brought considerable danger to the saints making their way between various monasteries of Wales, Cornwall, Brittany and Ireland or voyaging on missionary expeditions.

The Atlantic coastline of these regions is exposed to the prevailing southwesterly gales that originate far out in the Atlantic, batter the small harbours and beaches, and endanger any shipping unfortunate enough to be caught too far from shelter. The other challenge arises from the high tidal range caused by the compression of the incoming flood tides in St George's Channel and then in the narrowing Bristol Channel. This is shown by the average difference in the height of sea level between the highest and lowest tides at Milford Haven being 6.3 metres, but at Avonmouth a massive 12.2 metres. This rise and fall, occurring over a twelve-hour cycle, produces strong tidal streams which can sweep a small boat under oars or sail far upstream or out to sea, depending on whether the tide is flooding or ebbing. The danger for the Celtic saints arose from the possibility of a strong flood tide overcoming the power of their sail or oars, and causing their boat to be grounded or wrecked on the Saxon-held shores of the upper Severn estuary. The ebb tide flowing out of the Bristol Channel could take them far to the west, leaving relatively sheltered waters and exposing them to potentially rougher seas.

Today's mariners intending to make passage through the area would probably begin their preparations by reading the relevant Admiralty charts and pilot books. The Lundy and Irish Sea Pilot warns: 'for most part the coast is subject to on-shore prevailing winds; harbours and anchorages that are often isolated and limited in their times of access, with approaches that can be difficult or even impossible in heavy weather.'

The Reeds Macmillan Nautical Almanac states: 'the North coast of Cornwall is very exposed. Yachts need to be sturdy and well-equipped since if bad weather develops no shelter may be at hand.'

On reaching the eastern shore of the Severn Estuary the Welsh and Irish monks would not be able to land at the havens of Portishead or Clevedon, for these former Roman-protected areas had become Saxon-held lands. Further west, the tidal rivers emptying into Barnstaple Bay offered favourable landings, particularly in the fourth and fifth centuries. The river Taw gave easy access far inland to Appledore and Barnstaple and the river Torridge to Bideford.

Unfortunately these ports also eventually fell into Saxon hands and the Britons were forced to land further west again at Watchet, which provided a well sheltered harbour but which had a dangerous tide race off Hartland Point. Successive Saxon advances forced the Britons further west still, to Padstow, which became the premier landing and embarkation point for Celtic traders and travellers of all kinds on the north Cornish coast.

At Padstow the river Camel gave excellent access to Bodmin Moor and an overland route to the headwaters of the river Fal, which allowed passage to Golant on the south coast of Cornwall from where sea-going departures to Brittany could be obtained. Even today Golant is accessible from the sea up an unmarked channel of the Fal, although the major commercial port has now moved to the mouth of the river at Falmouth, still busy with its export trade of China clay. In the days of the saints the main embarkation point would have been from Golant, where ships carried ingots of tin for trading on the continent. Over a thousand years earlier the Celtic tribes had used this route to carry the same cargo for trading with the Phoenicians at St Michael's Mount on the south Cornish coast. The same activity was noted by Pytheas in around 3 BC, although at that time the continental traders may have been Greek.

Eventually two main trans-peninsula routes were used by saints travelling between Gaul and Wales or Ireland. The routes linked the north coast ports serving voyagers to Wales and Ireland and the south coast ports to Gaul. The two routes followed tracks from Harlyn Bay to Fowey, or St Ives to St Michael's Mount.

St Sulien (sixth century)

Voyages: Brittany – Tywyn – Bardsey Island – Menai Strait – Llandrillo-yn-Rhos – Corwen, River Dee – Porth-clais, southern Wales – Cornwall – Brittany.

Sulien was one of the monks who landed with Cadfan's party at Tywyn in Cardigan Bay but although he was a Breton he was related to King Cunedda and was also a cousin of St David. He worked energetically in west and mid Wales, founding a number of churches in Dyfed and Powys. He also voyaged northwards along the Welsh coast, calling at Bardsey and continuing through the Menai Strait to sail eastwards along the coast of northern Wales, resting at Llandrillo-yn-Rhos near Colwyn Bay. Continuing eastwards, Sulien, who was also accompanied by his fellow Breton monk St Mael, entered the Dee estuary and navigated inland where both saints have dedications at Corwen and Cwm in Denbighshire.

Sulien then made a return voyage to southwest Wales, most probably staying with his cousin St David at Menevia, before crossing the Bristol Channel for Cornwall. Here he founded the church at Luxulyan, although St Juliot is now its patron saint. Sulien then departed Cornwall to return to Brittany, where he had a cult following.

St Decuman (sixth century)

Voyages: Rhoscrowther – Flat Holm Island – Steep Holm Island – Watchet – Rhoscrowther.

Decuman was a Welsh monk who left Rhoscrowther (Llandegyman) in Pembrokeshire, near the site of the present-day oil refinery, to sail in his coracle to Watchet on the north Somerset coast and then on to Dunster. He had to voyage across the Severn Estuary, with its 12.2 metre tidal range and many hazards for mariners. There are many drying banks and shoals upon which ships can founder, such as the Mixon shoals off the Mumbles, or the Scarweather Sands and Nash Sands, which are typical of shoals that are covered at high tide but at low water dry out to a height of three metres. Any vessel unfortunate enough to become stranded on them faces a very uncertain fate.

Decuman would have made use of the havens provided by the islands of Flat Holm and Steep Holm, which are easily visible from the Welsh and English coast, and which provide some shelter and refuge. These were visited by Celtic saints, and St Gildas lived as a hermit on Flat Holm for seven years.

Decuman could also have sheltered at the most well-known island in the Severn Estuary, Lundy Island, which lies ten miles north of Hartland Point off the north Devon coast. Lundy is only 2.5 miles long and 0.75 miles wide, with steep granite cliffs rising to 120 metres in places, but would still have provided a safe approach for anchorage and shelter at certain states of the tide. Small boats such as coracles could be pulled up on a shingle beach on the southeast of the island, where there is now a small church. Unfortunately Lundy is surrounded by tidal races and overfalls and can only be approached by small craft during periods of slack water. A race known as 'The White Horses' forms over the Stanley Bank to the northeast of the island, and similar races also extend one mile north of the island, just over one mile east of Rat Island, lying off Lundy's southeast point and one mile southwest of Lundy's Shutter Point.

St Decuman is patron saint of Watchet and St Decumans (Somerset), and there are dedications to him in Wells and Muchelney. He was engaged in converting the local people to Christianity, but unfortunately suffered the fate of many Celtic saints, when he met a violent end at the hands of pagan Saxons. He was attacked whilst at prayer in his church, and his head was cut off with a sword. Like Justinian, his headless body is reputed to have picked up its severed head, but carried it to a spring to be washed. The spring is now known as St Decumans Well, and is located on a hillside not far from St Decumans Church. The body, still carrying its head, then sailed back on a raft of twigs to Rhoscrowther in Wales, where it was laid to rest. A holy spring rose up at the final place of rest, and this second holy well is located just south of the church in the direction of Angle Bay.

St Brioc (died 510)

Voyages: Cardigan – Brittany – Cardigan – Cornwall – Brittany.

St Brioc was born near Cardigan in south-western Wales. His Life, written in the twelfth century, states that he was educated in Gaul, from where he returned to the Cardigan area to found a monastery at Llandyfriog. He also has dedications in south-eastern Wales and in Cornwall, where he is known as St Breock. He may well have taken a land route to Cornwall as indicated by his churches there at St Briavels and St Breoke. From Cornwall he made his way to Gaul, where he is known as St Brieuc and has thirteen churches to his name, mainly in north Brittany and the Morbihan. He died in Brittany and, as his church at St-Brieuc was on the coast and exposed to Viking raiders, his remains were taken to Angers for safety, although in 1210 his neck bones, two ribs and an arm were returned to the church of St-Brieuc. He was renowned for his great charity, and so became the patron saint of purse makers.

St Cadog (died 560)

Voyages: Llancarfan – Harlyn Bay – Falmouth

St Cadog was born in southern Wales, either at Fochriw at the head of the Rhymney Valley in Glamorgan, or at Newport, Gwent, and was the son of Gwynlliw, King of Gwent and St Gwladys, daughter of King Brychan. He was educated by Illtud at Llanilltud Fawr and by Tathan at Caerwent. He became the Abbot of Llancarfan on the coast of south Glamorgan, which also became a highly regarded centre of learning. He founded many churches in south Wales and has dedications in churches in south-eastern Wales: at Llangattock in Gwent; on the Gower Peninsula; in the Vale of Glamorgan around Llancarfan; at former Roman military communities at Gelligaer, situated about fifteen miles inland along the Rhymney Valley; and at Caerleon on the river Usk. Cadog voyaged to Ireland with Gildas, and on his return from his Irish missionary work he sailed to Cornwall, where he followed a trans-peninsula way from Harlyn Bay, where there is a ruined chapel to his name, to St Just in Roseland, where a nearby holy well is dedicated to him. Near the river Fal is a second holy well at Venton Gassick, which in 1230 was called Fenton Cadog. From the Fal estuary Cadog joined a ship bound for Gaul, and he lived as a hermit at Etel in Brittany. Cadog eventually returned to his monastery at Llancarfan, where he suffered a violent end to his life during an attack by pagans, most probably sea-borne Saxon raiders. An alternative legend tells of him travelling from Brittany to Benevento in Italy where he was martyred. Legend also refers to him as a cousin of King Arthur and one of two knights charged with protection of the Holy Grail.

St Petrog (died 564)

Voyages: Wales – Ireland – Llanbedrog – Verwig, River Teifi; St Petrox – Timberscombe, Somerset – Haylemouth – Padstow – Rome – Palestine – India – Cornwall

Petrog was born in southern Wales and was the son of King Glywys of Glamorgan and Gwent. He trained for his monastic life in Ireland, where he remained for twenty-six years. He returned to Wales, where he has dedications at Llanbedrog in Llŷn; at Ferwig near the Teifi estuary; and St Petrox in south Pembrokeshire. He then made a voyage similar to that of Decuman, departing from southern Wales but landing at Timberscombe near Watchet in north Somerset, before voyaging further south along the peninsula to land at Haylemouth. From there he embarked on a pilgrimage to Rome, voyaging along the western sea routes to the Mediterranean. Petrog may have returned from this voyage to the Hayle estuary before a further coastal passage along the north Cornish coast to Padstow and the monastery of Lanwethinoc, where he found St Samson, also known in Cornwall as St Wethenoc, leading the religious community. There was a dispute between the two saints, and Samson departed for Fowey, leaving Petrog to build a monastery at Padstow and nearby Little Petherick.

An alternative account from the Vita Petroci tells of Petrog returning from Ireland after a period of twenty years to Cornwall, rather than Wales, where he landed at the mouth of the river Camel near the ancient port of Trebetherick, close to Padstow. This voyage was completed in the same vessel in which Petrog had sailed to Ireland, and appears to have been an exhilarating passage, for the account states '... the sails spread, the ship was borne along by the fear of God and with great rapidity although the winds were adverse'. From here the two legends appear to coincide with Petrog then founding the monastery at Lanwethinoc. He founded a further monastery at Little Petherick (Nanceverton) where he also built a mill. Seventeen churches are dedicated to him in Devon and six in Cornwall. This legend also tells that a prophecy he gave failed: during a miserable period of continuous rain he said it would end the following day, but it did not. After this failure he decided he had to make a long pilgrimage. He boarded a ship and sailed to Rome, and travelled on to Jerusalem and India. Here a silver globe drifted across the water to where he stood on a beach. He left his sheepskin coat and staff on the shore and embarked in the silver globe, which took him to an island. He remained on the island for seven years eating only a single fish that resurrected itself each day so that he was never short of food. The silver globe then re-appeared and took him back to the mainland where he found a wolf guarding his coat and staff. He returned to Cornwall, taking the wolf with him, which is why he is always portrayed accompanied by a wolf. Petrog also worked in Brittany, where he is known as St Perreuse, and where eight churches or chapels are dedicated to him.

At the Celtic monasteries of Cornwall, it is archaeological finds relating in particular to Petrog that help in establishing the cultural connections with Gaul, Ireland and the Mediterranean. Tintagel, at 470, is the oldest accurately dated monastery in Britain, and here pottery shards bearing Christian symbols have been unearthed and identified as being similar to examples found in Egypt and Tunisia. A fifth-century pottery fragment found in Cornwall and displaying a particular style of the cross is similar to examples found at St Blaize, Marseilles, and four glass shards are not of western Roman Britain origin, but are most probably eastern. Petrog's monastery and also Castle Dore have material similar to St Mochaoi's monastery in Strangford Loch, Ireland, and Dinas Emrys hill fort in Caernarfonshire; while Tintagel pottery is also found at Dinas Powys in southern Wales. Garryduff in County Cork also has Egyptian glass similar to that found in Cornwall.

Other Welsh saints from south-western Wales with dedications in Cornwall are St Gwybert; St Meugan (St Mawgan), who is also dedicated at Ruthin in northern Wales; Congar; Hernin, and Collen, some of whom also have churches in Devon and Somerset. The dedications to these saints in Somerset indicates that the shorter estuary crossing was available at times, although the major number of dedications to Celtic saints are in the areas accessed from the estuaries of the Gannel and Camel and in the Fowey area, suggesting that the longer, outer crossing of the Bristol Channel was generally necessary.

Chapter 6

İRELAND, THE İRİSH SEA AND THE ATLANTIC OCEAN.

Wondrous the warriors who abode in Hi
Thrice fifty in monastic rule
With their boats along the main sea
Three score men a rowing.

From *The Book of Lismore*

Many of the Irish saints were frequent, almost compulsive voyagers. Their travels took them northwards through the dangerous and inhospitable waters of the Atlantic Ocean and the Icelandic Sea to reach areas such as the Faroe Islands, Greenland, Iceland, Newfoundland, and Labrador. Their small, sturdy curraghs sailed the length of Britain's coastline and beyond, to the coast of western Europe, the Mediterranean and as far south as the Azores. Irish saints were also more active than those from any other nation in navigating the major rivers such as the Seine, the Loire and the Rhine, to take their message of Celtic Christianity to the pagan tribes of central Europe. The seamanship and navigation of the Irish saints was second to none, whether they voyaged in their native Irish-built curraghs powered by sail and oars in heavy timbered flat-bottomed estuary ships, or in sea-going clench-built trading ships.

Hardly any part of the western sea routes and river systems escaped the influence of Irish saints following their compulsion for pilgrimage and teaching. Whereas the other British saints, particularly the Welsh, tended to work among their fellow Celts, the Irish worked actively and courageously among the Picts, Saxons, Jutes and other pagan Germanic tribes, in Britain and on the continent. They founded teaching monasteries wherever they could, and a significant number of monasteries or communities in Europe are a testament to their success.

Most voyages were with a specific destination in mind, and some were recorded in great detail, while other voyages resulted from monks committing themselves to the vagaries of the sea and the weather. An example of the latter kind of voyage is given by the three Irish saints who departed their native shore in a curragh with a supply of food and no more wish than 'to go into exile for love of God – they cared not whither'. They were washed up on the western shore of Britain, probably Wales or Cornwall, where their exploit was duly recorded by a scribe of the local chieftain.

The major voyaging routes of the Irish Saints were across the Irish Sea from the south of Ireland to Wales and Cornwall – a distance of about sixty to ninety miles depending on the precise course chosen – or across the narrow North Channel from north-eastern Ireland to Scotland, where the passage from Bangor to Portpatrick is only eighteen miles, or from Rathlin Island off Antrim's coast to Scotland's Mull of Kintyre, which is just eleven miles.

However, a study of the tidal stream charts of the northern Irish Sea gives a hint of the dangers presented to a small sailing or rowing boat. The south-eastern-going flood-tide surging into the Irish Sea through the north Channel can reach up to 8 knots – a rate that would overwhelm any boat likely to be used by Celtic saints. Their vessels would be swept far to the south, so that the seemingly short passage could become an extended voyage of several days rather than a matter of hours. Even if the mariner was able to use a following favourable wind to push his ship against the tide and towards his destination he could experience the very unpleasant sea conditions caused by a 'wind over tide' situation, where the opposing forces of tide and wind create tumultuous, short, choppy waves against which progress would be slow, uncomfortable and dangerous. The north-western flowing ebb tide is as ferocious as the flood, and an even greater problem is that the ship would be swept northwards, out of the shelter of the Irish Sea and into the dangerous overfalls and whirlpools of the Scottish Western Isles. The story of St Cormac, who, according to Adomnan, was swept northwards for 'fourteen days and fourteen nights beyond the limit of human endurance', is an indication of the perils that can befall the seafarer making the 'short' crossing from Ireland to Scotland.

Those monks who voyaged among the lochs, sounds and islands of Scotland's west coast were not making particularly long voyages and so had no need to use advanced navigational techniques, but they did need pilotage skills of the highest order, and a full understanding of the tidal patterns. Tidal streams become much stronger when the flow of the tides is restricted or compressed, such as off headlands or narrow channels – of which there are many off western Scotland. Overfalls (rough turbulent water) can form frequently at the seaward end of narrow sounds or channels, and also where two tidal streams meet – another common condition of this voyaging area. The geography and geology of the region consists of steep-sided sounds, prominent headlands, an uneven sea bed, and towering stacks and mountains, which can provide prominent navigation markers but can also create treacherous sea states and weather. Normally, an island to the windward of a boat can provide shelter in its lee, but the steep, rugged nature of many of the Scottish islands can actually create turbulent gusts on the leeward side, or even deflections of wind from different directions. In summer, a hot, windless day can result in a strong katabatic wind (created by cold wind tumbling down a steep slope) early the following morning. Frequently heavy precipitation over the steep, high hills and islands can result in a significant amount of erosion, and fast-running rivers, burns and streams build up into a torrent carrying debris into the sounds, creating shallow banks and shoals of pebbles and sand to impede the unwary sailor. The saints sailing regularly among the islands would need to build up a sound knowledge of the tidal streams and pilotage information, such as depth of water, reefs and significant landmarks to steer by.

For the saints the longer, southern crossing of the southern Irish Sea also entailed strong tides, but had the advantage of more 'sea room' so that there was less danger of being swept on to a dangerous shore. Some of the Irish voyagers heading for the Welsh or Cornish coasts could break their journey at the Isle of Man, a vibrant centre of Christianity with a number of natural harbours and ports of refuge. Another advantage of the longer southern passage was that the greater length of the voyage here also allowed time for the twelve-hourly rhythm of successive tides to be set off against each other so that the navigator's course would remain true. A ship maintaining its heading on a southerly course from the Isle of Man to Holyhead on Môn could experience six hours of flood tide pushing it eastwards, followed by six hours of ebb tide pushing it back westwards for the same distance, so that after a twelve-hour voyage the ship would be back on its southerly track. During this period of the tidal stream deflecting the ship east then west a steady southwards progress would still have been maintained, bringing the destination closer.

Although many of the voyages of the Irish saints were confined to the Irish Sea, some of the voyages to the Western Isles of Scotland were extended further northwards to the Shetland, Orkney and Faroe Isles – some even to Iceland, Greenland and Labrador, while those leaving the southern Irish Sea could proceed onwards to Brittany, Spain and the Azores.

The Irish saints were also the most adventurous, brave and determined in their exploitation of the continental river systems; the voyages of men such as Columbanus and Gall, who navigated the rivers, are recounted in a later chapter.

SIGNIFICANT IRISH MONASTERIES AND IRISH SEA ROUTES

Bangor

Derry

Armagh

Kells

Aran Is.

Clonard

Inis Carthaig

St Columba (Colm Cille) (521 – 597)

Voyages: Garten – Donegal – Moville – Clonard – Derry – Durrow – Kells – Howth – Iona – Tiree – the Scottish Highlands and east coast.

Columba, known in Irish as Colm Cille, the Dove of the Church, like many of the Celtic saints, was the son of a royal family. He was born in Donegal in 521, where his father was chieftain of the Ui Neill clan, and his mother was from the ruling house of Leinster. He trained as a monk under Finnian of Moville and then Finnian of Clonard, and founded monasteries at Derry and Durrow. The king of Dalriada gave him the island of Iona, just south of Mull, on which to build another monastery, and in 565 he departed Ireland to sail there. Before he left he had been engaged in a fierce dispute with Finnian of Moville from whom he had borrowed a rare and beautiful book which Finnian had brought back from Italy. Initially Columba was not permitted to read the book, but after persistent requests he was allowed to study it. Unknown to Finnian, Columba made an unauthorised copy. When Finnian learned of the copy he demanded it be given him, but Columba refused. The dispute became so contentious that the matter was referred to Diarmit, King of Meath, for judgement, which was given as 'to every cow its calf, to every book its copy' – an instruction to Columba to give the copy to Finnian, its rightful owner. Columba must have been a stubborn man, for he still refused to give the copy to Finnian, and the dispute escalated into an armed conflict between the monasteries, which culminated in the battle of Cul Dreimhne when 'the men of Ulster slew 3,000 men of Meath'. Columba finally realised the human tragedy his actions had brought and in remorse decided to leave Ireland in penance, vowing to convert as many souls to Christianity as had been lost in the battle – hence his self-banishment to the Isle of Alba (Iona). However, other reasons more in keeping with a highly respected saint are given for his departure to Iona – such as his mission to convert the

Picts of western Scotland.

Columba wrote disconsolately about his departure from Ireland describing standing on the hill of Howth waiting for the coracle that would take him 'over the white haired sea' to 'Alba of the beetling brows'. He also describes his unhappiness in having to leave Ireland:

> Delightful to be on the hill of Howth
> Before going over the white haired sea:
> The dashing of waves against its face
> The bareness of its shores and of its border.
>
> Delightful to be on the hill of Howth
> After coming over the white blossomed sea:
> To be rowing one's little coracle
> Alas! On the wild-waved shore.
>
> Great is the speed of my coracle,
> And its stern turns upon Derry:
> Grievous is my errand over the main,
> Travelling to Alba of the beetling brows.

From Adomnan's *Vita Sancti Columbae* translated by Kuno Meyer)

The sea must have indeed been 'white haired' on that day because in the course of the voyage the boat took in a substantial amount of water and Columba instinctively lent a hand in bailing out the bilges. The crew was alarmed at this and asked him to stop, believing that it would be far more beneficial for them all if he prayed for the sea to become calmer. This must have been successful because Iona was safely reached.

Iona was a former druid's island only three miles long and lying off the south-western of the Island of Mull on the Scottish coast. The water between the west of the Ross of Mull and Iona is known as the Sound of Iona and the coastal rock there is a distinctive pink-coloured granite which overlooks beaches of startling white sand. The sound is very shallow in parts, with a shoal of shingle, sand and coral that impedes vessels at low tide. Today the island is a popular destination for visitors, and its cathedral is a majestic landmark.

After Columba and his twelve companions landed, they made Iona their permanent home and founded a religious settlement which prospered – at times it grew to a community of up to 150 monks. No cows were permitted because they would require women to tend them and women, in Columba's opinion, 'brought mischief'. The native women already on Iona were banished and none were allowed to return. This does not necessarily mean that Columba had a general disregard for women, for he was a very compassionate man, and Adomnan records that he gave solace and support to a grieving widow, as well as to other women in local communities requiring spiritual comfort. Vipers were also expelled from Iona for the safety of the monks.

Legend states that when Columba first landed on Iona he climbed to the highest point of the island to be sure that he could not see Ireland; he then buried the coracle in the pebbly beach of the island so that there could be no return. The burial of the coracle echoes the tradition of Irish invaders who burned their boats on landing on the beaches to signify that there was no going back. This is probably only a symbolic tale, for Columba was not marooned on Iona without a boat. In subsequent years he and his companion monks voyaged widely among the islands, sounds and sea lochs of western Scotland in their missionary work, and he also returned to Ireland for important religious occasions.

Columba made several visits to the pagan King Brude of the Picts at Inverness and was eventually successful in converting him. He founded two churches in the area. Inverness, on the east coast of Scotland, was reached from Iona by sailing eastwards along Mull's southern shore through the Firth of Lorn and into the sea loch of Loch

Linnhe. At the entrance to Loch Linnhe is the famous Isle of Lismore, separating the Loch into the Lynn of Morvern to the north and Lynn of Lorn to the south. At the north-east of Loch Linnhe is the town now known as Fort William, and here Columba's party disembarked for the brief overland trek to Loch Lochy, which was traversed by coracle before they once again disembarked for another short overland route and a further voyage along Loch Ness, and reached the Moray Firth at Inverness.

Columba also carried out a great deal of missionary work in the Irish-ruled part of Scotland and was successful in converting the Irish King Aidan of Dalriada. Subsequently he voyaged to the western islands such as Tiree, Coll, Lismore, and Islay; Loch Awe; and also penetrated the Scottish Highlands along the sea lochs and passes.

The Book of Lismore describes seafaring monks such as Columba in a reference to 'three score men rowing whose abode is in Hi' (Hinba Island):

> Wondrous the warriors who abode in Hi,
> Thrice fifty in monastic rule,
> With their boats along the main-sea,
> Three score men a-rowing.

One of Columba's sailing strategies is indicated in his chastisement of a younger monk who had sailed a direct course westwards from Iona to Tiree. Columba warned that a seafarer should not strain God's providence by choosing the longer sea passage when it was safer to make an 'island hopping' voyage of a number of shorter passages. This could have been accomplished by the younger monk making a circuitous series of short voyages from Iona to the Isle of Staffa, the Treshnish Isles, Coll, and then Tiree.

On a missionary expedition into the Pictish lands, one of Columba's brethren almost became a victim of the Loch Ness monster. Columba and his party came upon local inhabitants who were burying a man who had been killed by the monster. Columba wanted to cross the river Ness and asked one of his companion monks to swim into the Loch to retain a coracle that was adrift. Suddenly there was a great commotion as the monster returned and was seen making its way towards the swimming monk. Columba sprang into action and admonished the Loch Ness monster, which then swam away.

Another miraculous tale is associated with Loch Ness, where Columba's curragh was moored to the bank. A druid asked him when he was leaving, and Columba replied that it would be in three days. The druid said he would conjure up a storm to impede him. On the day of departure a great storm and darkness did arrive, and the crew of the boat were afraid to set sail. Columba took direct action and with his fellow monks fought to raise the sail against the wind. Columba prayed, and the wind dropped and then changed to a favourable direction for their departure, to the wonder of the crowds who witnessed the scene.

St Cormac – (Cormac the Sailor) (early sixth century).

Voyages: Clonard – Hebrides – Orkneys – Faroes – Iona (three voyages to 'the North')

Cormac, Abbot of Clonard, a great friend of Columba, was renowned for his learning, his creation of illuminated manuscripts, and for his voyaging from the northern Irish Sea to the Atlantic.

Few other voyagers would have set out with more determination than Cormac and his companions, who persevered in their quest to discover a 'Diseart' with at least three voyages northwards from Ireland. They were several times waylaid by the strong Irish Sea currents and adverse winds, which took them far into northern waters. Their craft were seaworthy curraghs and kept them safely afloat, but in the *Vita Sancti Columbae* 'Life of St Columba' Adomnan records that during the second of Cormac's voyages he was blown so far north by southerly winds that he landed among the Pictish-ruled Orkney Islands. Had it not been for

Columba, who had previously requested King Brude of Inverness, the King of the Picts, to issue instructions for the safety of all saints travelling in northern waters, he and his companions would possibly have met a brutal end.

On his third voyage across the Irish Sea, Cormac was again blown far to the north by persistent southerly winds, and Adomnan recounts that 'the craft was under full sail for fourteen summer days and nights, holding a straight course to the north until he seemed to pass beyond the limits of human journeying and beyond the hope of return'.

This experience was fully understood by further generations of sailors who experienced the helplessness of being driven off their course by a strong wind, but a later part of Adomnan's account might, at first, cause a slight frown of scepticism. He claims that:

> after the tenth hour of the fourteenth day dangers of a formidable and insurmountable kind presented themselves. Cormac and his fellow monks found their vessel attacked by a multitude of monsters which had never been seen before. They were like insects which covered the sea in swarms and struck against the keel and sides, prow and stern of the vessel, so violently that it seemed they would penetrate the leather covering of the ship. The monsters could not fly but could swim and were about the size of frogs which crowded up to the handles of the oars where they stung the monks, leaving them in great pain and shedding copious tears in their fear.

It is probably the account of Cormac or one of his companions referring to the painful stings that caused the writer, Adomnan, to use the term 'insects'. What was described was clearly outside the normal experience of that time, and Adomnan was struggling to find appropriate language to record what he believed had been experienced. However, once the anomalous terms of 'insects' and 'monsters' are removed and the other descriptive terms are considered, it is clear that the unfortunate mariners had found themselves sailing through a large shoal of stinging jellyfish, which are not normally found in the cold northern waters but on this occasion were perhaps carried north by a warm current or the prolonged southerly winds. It may have appeared to them that the 'monsters' were attempting to penetrate the leather hull or climb up the oars to attack them, but the jellyfish were probably being pushed against the hull by wave action and entangled their tentacles around the oars and bare arms of the rowers. Adomnan also records that while this drama was unfolding, the plight of Cormac and his companions was known to Columba, who was with them in spirit. Columba exhorted his fellow monks on Iona to pray to God to cause the wind that was blowing from the south and driving Cormac 'beyond the limits of human journeying' to cease, and to blow from the north, and so deliver Cormac's ship from danger. This duly happened and with the change in prevailing wind Cormac made it safely to Iona where the two saints met.

In Cormac's voyaging into these northern waters it is likely that in addition to the Orkneys he also visited the Shetlands and possibly the Faroes. In 825 Dicuil, an Irish monk at the Carolingian court in France, wrote *Liber de Mensura orbis Terrae* (Geography of the World) in which he gave details of islands to the north of Britain (probably the Faroes), and also the island of Thule, (probably Iceland), where Irish saints had lived since 700. Dicuil had spoken to monks with first-hand knowledge of these voyages to the far north. He observes:

> There are many other islands in the ocean to the north of Britain and on these islands are hermits who sailed from our Scotia [Ireland] and have lived there for a hundred years but even as they have been constantly uninhabited since the world's beginning, so now, because of Norse pirates they are empty of anchorites but full of innumerable sheep and a great many different kinds of

sea fowl. I have never found these islands mentioned in the books of scholars.

There are Scandinavian accounts of the first Norsemen reaching Iceland to find Christian Irish people there, who moved off, leaving their books, bells and crosiers behind. The naming of localities on Iceland suggests these Irish settlements were on the southeast of the island. The reference to the Irish Christians having 'moved off' is probably a euphemism cloaking a more brutal end to the monks' existence there – it is not likely they would have voluntarily abandoned their books, bells and crosiers to simply move away. Pagan Norsemen were not known for their tolerance of Christian monks.

St Cainnech (Kenneth) (525 – 600)

**Voyages: Maghera, County Derry – Llancarfan, Wales –
Isle of Monahincha, County Tipperary – Mull –
Iona – Tiree – Coll – South Uist – Islay – Lismore –
Kenneth Island – Faroes – Kennoway and
St Andrews, Fife – Laggan-Kenny –
Loch Laggan – Inverness – Kilkenny West,
County Westmeath – Kilkenny, River Nore.**

St Cainnech was a contemporary of Columba, Finnian, Ciaran of Clonmacnois, Cormac the Sailor, and Brendan the Navigator, and although from a poor family he was able to pursue his ambition to become a priest. His first voyage was across the south Irish Sea, probably from a port in the Wexford area to southeast Wales, where he trained under St Cadog at his teaching monastery of Llancarfan on the north shore of the Severn Estuary.

On returning to Ireland Cainnech became interested in the work undertaken by Columba to convert the Pictish kingdoms of Scotland, and he therefore joined him on his missionary expeditions there. Columba was initially unsuccessful in his approach to King Brude, King of the Picts, but persevered to secure a second audience at Brude's castle at Inverness – an audience to which he invited Cainnech and Comgall, both of whom were Pictish speakers. This second meeting was successful, and this and a further meeting enabled Columba to obtain, amongst other things, a grant of protection of all Christian monks travelling by sea through Brude's kingdom. Cainnech, who had also forged a good personal relationship with King Brude, then voyaged further north from Inverness on Scotland's east coast to the 'Island of Birds' in the Faroe Islands – an island also visited by his contemporary Brendan the Navigator (whose momentous voyage is discussed later in the chapter).

After the Faroe Isles Cainnech sailed southwestwards, passing along the northern coast of mainland Scotland and making a landfall in the Western Isles. Cainnech founded a church on the island of Tiree, and also worshipped on the neighbouring Isle of Coll. The naming of Inch Kenneth, a small crescent-shaped island off the west coast of Mull and to the northeast of Iona, is also an indication of his association with that group of islands. His island voyages then took him to South Uist, the large Isle of Mull, and Columba's monastery on Iona, which lies just to the south. In his voyages between Iona and Ireland, Cainnech also rested at Islay and Lismore.

During his tireless work amongst the Picts, Cainnech spent time resting in retreat at a cell in Glen Coe. This journey was made by boat from Tiree, by a passage through the Sound of Mull and entrance into Loch Linnhe; he disembarked on the eastern shore at Ballachulish at the entrance of Loch Leven and Glen Coe itself. A voyage northeastwards along Loch Linnhe and through the Corran narrows was also the access route through the Highlands to northeastern Scotland – a route that today carries the Caledonian Canal linking the Irish Sea to the North Sea. This saved the long, exposed sea passage along the north coast of Scotland. Cainnech used this route, which at the time would have been a combination of voyaging by curragh along the lochs and short overland treks, to found churches at

**THE ROUTES OF STS CAINNECH (KENNETH)
AND COLMCILLE (COLUMBA) IN SCOTLAND**

FAROE ISLES

SHETLAND

ORKNEY

Inverness

Coll

Tiree

Loch Linnhe

Treshnish
Isles

Iona

Mull

Lismore

St. Andrews

Whithorn

locations such as Laggan Kenny on Loch Laggan within Brude's Pictish kingdom.

Cainnech also used a combination of trekking and loch voyaging to reach south-eastern Scotland; he founded a church at Kennoway, on Largo Bay, Fife, and at nearby St Andrews on the east coast, just south of the Tay estuary, where his monastery was known as Kil-Rigmond. Once again, the access from Cainnech's base on the west-coast islands of Iona or Tiree was by sea to Loch Linnhe, passing into Loch Leven and trekking over the pass of Glen Coe, and across the bleak Rannoch Moor, to take to a coracle again to sail along Loch Laidon, Loch Rannoch and Loch Tummel, where he would follow the river Tummel, passing Pitlochry, to join the Tay and continue downstream to reach the sea at the Firth of Tay. He also had available to him a more southerly route through the Grampian Mountains, by leaving Rannoch Moor to negotiate Glen Dochart and sail along Loch Tay and its river. Both options allowed him to pick up the river Tay which provided access to the coast of Fife.

On returning to Ireland, Cainnech founded further monasteries, and was granted land to build a church alongside the river Nore where the town of Kilkenny is now sited. His retreat in Ireland was also on an island, this time not offshore, but in a lake: it was known as the Isle of Monahincha, near Roscrea, in County Tipperary. There were no deep waters surrounding this retreat, and no boat is required to reach the island today because the lake has now dried out.

St Enda (died 530)

Voyages: Howth – Whithorn – Drogheda – Aran Islands

Enda was another voyaging Irish monk, a member of a royal family who surrendered his inheritance to lead a life in the service of the church. His early travels led him from his church at Killany, between Dundalk and Carrickmacross on the southeast coast of Ireland, across the Irish Sea by curragh to the Isle of Whithorn in Galloway, Scotland, to attend Ninian's monastery known as 'Candida Casa'. After his return voyage to Ireland he travelled overland and by river to Galway, from where he embarked on the short passage to Inishmore in the Aran Islands, off Galway, on Ireland's west coast.

While the voyages to Whithorn across the northern Irish sea were by the conventional vessels of the time – leather-hulled curraghs – his landing on Aran was designed to impress the local pagan chieftain, Corban. Legend recounts that in order to make such an impression Enda declined to undertake the passage in the offered curragh, and instead voyaged over the waves on a large stone. This stone still lies on the beach near the monastic settlement and is known locally as the 'the Curragh Stone' or 'the saint's boat'.

Enda's monastic settlement on Inishmore was highly acclaimed and was visited by many illustrious saints, including Ciaran, Columba, Finnian of Moville and Finnian of Clonard, and the islands became known as 'Aran of the Saints'. St Brendan visited Enda at Aran to discuss his proposed voyage into the far north, for Enda was knowledgeable about the various Irish monastic settlements lying in the high latitudes.

There are many Christian monuments, cells and churches located over the Aran Islands, particularly Inishmore: at the western end of the island is the site known as 'The Seven Churches' and at the eastern end, Killeany. Sites bearing the names 'Teampaill' and 'Teighleach' have specific religious designations and are found throughout the islands, confirming their Christian origins.

St Patrick (fourth/fifth century)
Voyages: Solway Firth – Northern Ireland – Gaul – Mediterranean Islands – Wales – Ireland; also Auxerre, Lerins, Inver-Cloptha, Armagh.

Although primarily associated with Ireland, St Patrick was not an Irishman but probably born in 389 in a Roman town somewhere on the west coast of mainland Britain, between the estuaries of the Severn and the Clyde. The precise location is not known but Birdoswald – near Carlisle, and at the western end of Hadrian's Wall in Cumbria – has been proposed as a likely location, despite claims that he may have been of Welsh origin. The evidence indicates the northern England origin to be more likely. St Patrick's original, Roman name was Sucat; he was the son of Calpurnius, who held the administrative position of a decurion or deacon. St Patrick would therefore have had a formal Roman upbringing and classical education. Patrick's grandfather was a priest and his mother is recorded in some sources as being a sister of Martin of Tours, which may have been significant in his later journeys in Gaul.

St Patrick's first experience of a sea voyage at the age of sixteen was an unpleasant one: he was in the unfortunate and uncomfortable position of being a securely bound captive, bundled with many other victims into the bottom of a large Irish curragh, a fast, easily manoeuvred vessel capable of making lightning raids along the north British coastline. This type of vessel could be easily rowed if the wind dropped, and could also be pulled quietly up onto a beach to allow a raiding party to disembark before any alarm was raised. Patrick was kidnapped by Irish raiders and taken to Ireland where he was sold as a slave. For the next six years he was put to work tending sheep at Slemish Mountain, County Antrim, for a man named Milchu. It was here that he experienced a dream in which he was told that he should escape and make his way to a ship that was 200,000 paces distant, and which was about to depart. St Patrick did escape and made his way to a major trading port in the south, possibly to Howth, where he was able to secure passage on a merchant ship. This ship carried hunting dogs amongst the cargo of exports. The ship was at sea for three or four days, which suggests a voyage to Gaul. This also fits the international maritime trading pattern of the time.

This voyage would be fairly typical of the import/export trade around northern Europe, where merchants used heavily-built Romano-Celtic vessels for trading fur, hides, cattle, wine, grain, dogs, wool, pottery, metal weapons and domestic goods between the continent and the British Isles. These vessels were sturdy planked boats built on heavy oak frames, fastened together with iron nails, with a deck and a lined hold for carrying cargo, as well as a cabin to provide shelter for the crew – quite different to the curragh in which Patrick first crossed the Irish Sea. However his second experience of a voyage was not without incident: during a storm, as the ship approached its destination, it was wrecked on the western coast of Gaul – possibly in the region of Nantes, which is known to have been a trading port from which ships sailed directly to Ireland. Patrick and other survivors then wandered through the area until they were given shelter at a religious settlement. As an educated Romano-Briton brought up in a family of some religious and civic stature, possibly with a family relationship with Martin of Tours on his mother's side, Patrick was able to establish himself in Gaul.

In Gaul he voyaged along the navigable rivers – safer routes than the former Roman highways, which had become dangerous for unprotected travellers. The river boats were heavy flat barges poled or towed against the sluggish currents of the river's lower reaches, and passengers would transfer to vessels of a lighter construction, rowed by a dozen or so men, as they progressed inland and encountered faster currents and shoals.

St Patrick is likely to have navigated the Loire, the Saône and the Yonne, possibly visiting the monastery founded by St Martin on the Loire, and the monastery of Germanus of Auxerre on the banks of the Yonne, where he remained for some time before he made an upstream navigation and overland trek to the headwaters of the Rhône. This arterial waterway then took him swiftly downstream to reach the

Mediterranean, where a sea-going vessel departing the ancient Greek port of Massalia (Marseilles) gave him a coastal passage eastwards. Passing Toulon and the Isles de Hyers, he made landfall at the monastery of Honorat on the Isle de Lerins, near Cannes.

From Lerins, St Patrick voyaged further into the Mediterranean and was particularly active on the many islands of the Tyrrhenian Sea, ringed by the large islands of Sardinia and Corsica to the west, the Italian mainland with its many small offshore islands to the east, and Sicily to the south.

In 432 St Patrick was sent by the Pope as a missionary bishop to Ireland and his voyage was probably on a large, sturdily-built trading ship that sailed directly out of the Mediterranean and then took a bearing north to follow the Pole star. He reached Ireland during an Easter high tide and sailed up Strangford Lough to land at the mouth of the river Slaney, where he began preaching to the people in the area. A local chieftain was impressed at Patrick's teaching and gave him a barn (sabball) to shelter in whilst he remained in the locality. The site of the barn now has a sign proclaiming it to be 'The First Ecclesiastical Site in Ireland'. In 433 St Patrick and his followers visited Tara, the court of Laoghaire, the High King of Ireland, where he overcame the attempts of the druids who served the royal family to discredit him, and was granted the king's permission to preach his new religion under royal protection throughout the land.

St Patrick had further success in his missionary work when, in 450, he visited Aengus, King of Munster, at the Rock of Cashel, County Tipperary, and converted him to Christianity. Legend says that while St Patrick was baptising Aengus he inadvertently drove the spike of his crozier through the King's foot. Aengus bore the painful wound in silence and when St Patrick noticed the bleeding at the end of the ceremony he asked him why he had not spoken up. Aengus replied that he thought it was part of the ceremony.

Clearly this mishap did not impede St Patrick's influence

in the northern part of the country, and in 455 he founded a church at Armagh on a hill known as Druim Saileach (Sallow Ridge), the site of the current Church of Ireland cathedral. He was energetic in his endeavours to counter pagan beliefs, including sun worship, and to restore an orthodox Roman Christianity in a form that appealed to the Celtic population. As his foundation in Ireland grew stronger, St Patrick made numerous Irish Sea voyages from Ireland's east coast to the ports of south-western and northern Wales. Here his missionary work among his fellow Celts resulted in a legacy of dedications in Pembrokeshire and on Môn, where a church dedicated to him stands in the village of Llanbadrig. Legend tells that this church was founded by Patrick as thanks to God for being saved when his ship foundered on a small rocky island known as Middle Mouse, which lies off Cemaes Bay. There are also dedications to St Patrick in a number of English churches.

Ciaran of Clonmacnois (512 – 545)

Voyages: Clonard – Enda (Isle of Aran) – Scattery Island – Clonmacnois (Shannon)

Ciaran of Clonmacnois, the son of a carpenter, studied at Clonard under Finnian and then in around 534 visited St Enda's monastery on Inishmore, where he was ordained a priest. He left for Senan on Scattery Island in 541 and subsequently established his own monastery at Clonmacnois on the Shannon in County Offaly, along with ten companions. Unfortunately he died within a year at the age of thirty-three. One account of the time suggested that other Irish saints (apart from Columba) were so jealous of Ciaran's achievements that they prayed for him to die young. Clonmacnois became one of the most important monasteries and learning centres in Ireland. There are notable ruins there and it remains one of the best preserved sites in Ireland. The monastery is famed for its high crosses, and also has two round towers and the remains of six churches.

Ninian (fifth century)

Voyages: Tours – River Loire – Guernsey – Porth Clais, Pembrokeshire – Howth – Bangor (Northern Ireland) – St Ninian's Isle – Whithorn

Ninian was one of Britain's first bishops. He was born in around 360 AD into a noble Romano-British family in the Solway Firth. He voyaged from Scotland on a pilgrimage to Rome, and on his return stayed with Martin of Tours on the Loire in Gaul, where he became a disciple. On his return to Britain he set up a monastery and school at the Isle of Whithorn in Galloway in 397. Whithorn is one of the oldest centres of Christian worship in Britain and was a popular destination on the western sea routes: lying at the southern end of the Mull of Galloway, it formed a natural landing place for vessels using the tides to sail northwards through the Irish Sea.

Whithorn is not an island but stands on a promontory on which, just to the east of the harbour, the conspicuous white, square St Ninian's Tower now stands as a warning beacon to mariners, for there is a reef of rocks lying just off this point. The remains of St Ninian's chapel are also nearby. There are archaeological links between the site and the Mediterranean and Near East and, unusually, the church was painted white. Bede called Whithorn '*Ad Candidum Casa*' – meaning the 'White House'. The white-painted masonry indicates that an earlier church may have been founded on the site of Candida Casa by missionaries from Palestine and Egypt. Ninian died in 432 after he had also founded a cult in south Wales.

St Brendan (486 – 575)

Voyages: Clonfert – Brandon Creek, County Kerry – Inishmore (Isles of Arran) – Inishmurray – Tory Island – Inishea – Inishglora – Hebrides – Orkney – Shetland – Hebrides – Faroes (Isle of Sheep) – Southern Iceland (Fiery Island) – Mykines or Vagar (Paradise of Birds) –

Newfoundland – St Ailbe's Community – return route to Ireland

One of the greatest of the Irish seafaring monks was Brendan, the Abbot of Clonfert, who had three thousand monks in his care. Whilst at Clonfert, Brendan was visited by the monk Barrind, who told him that when he had visited St Mernoc, the abbot of a monastery on an island to the north, the two of them, Barrind and Mernoc, had sailed to the 'Promised Land of the Saints'. Intrigued, Brendan wanted to see this special place himself, and he therefore visited St Enda of Inishmore (the Aran Isles) for advice and to obtain a blessing for himself and fourteen companion monks to search for this Promised Land. Leaving Brandon Creek in County Kerry, Brendan sailed northwards up the west coast of Ireland in a curragh. It was constructed of leather hides tanned with oak bark, which was stretched and stitched over a frame of ash, with oak gunwales. The boat had a mast of ash and sail of hide, as well as oars for each crew member.

Brendan and his party were away for two years. The voyage took them along the western shore of Ireland where they halted at the monasteries at Inishmurray, Tory Island, Inishea and Inishglora (this last one had been founded by Brendan himself). The passage then continued northwards to the Hebrides, the Orkneys and the Shetland Isles, with a reversal back to the Hebrides, then on again to the 'Isle of Sheep' (the Faroe Isles) and 'The Paradise of Birds' (Mykines or Vangar), and back across the strait to the west of the Isle of Sheep. The voyage continued for a further three months to the island community of St Ailbe, where the travellers stayed to celebrate Christmas. It is not clear where Ailbe's community was. St Ailbe himself was born in south Wales but became an abbot of an Irish monastery. On leaving St Ailbe they sailed and rowed until Lent, by which time they had run out of food. After drifting for twenty days the wind blew them back to the Isle of Sheep, from where the voyagers retraced their route to 'The Paradise of Birds' to replenish their supplies.

Refreshed and revictualled, these adventurous sea-faring monks then resumed their voyage, departing to sail for a further forty days, during which time they saw whales and a flat island with three choirs on it. After sighting an 'Island of Fruit' they made their way back to Ailbe's community, once again to rest and replenish their supplies.

The voyaging resumed, and on leaving Ailbe for a second time they sailed further north than previously, encountering icebergs and, to their alarm, a smoking mountain that was covered in flames, and inhabited by smiths who hurled burning rocks and created a stench. This was quite clearly south Iceland during a volcanic phase. From here they returned again to the Isle of Sheep. They recorded their sighting of whales, birds, sheep, thick fog and an anchorite monk. It is not clear whether they landed on the coast of Labrador or Newfoundland (there is archaeological evidence of Ogham writing in Newfoundland, which indicates the early presence there of Irish monks).

After these extensive voyages in the inhospitable seas and weather of the high northern latitudes, which required seamanship, leadership and perseverance of the highest order, Brendan returned to Ireland without losing any of the loyal party who had embarked with him from Clonfert two years earlier.

The voyage is recorded as Navigato Sancti Brendani Abbotis in 120 Latin manuscripts. The details of the manuscripts have enabled historians to reconstruct this epic voyage, which was repeated by the explorer Tim Severin in 1976-7 and recounted in his own book entitled *The Brendan Voyage*. Although Severin encountered whales, he did not mistake one for an island and land on it to light a fire and cook a meal, as Brendan is alleged to have done.

The Severin boat was 36' by 8' and the design was reconstructed from historical detail by the respected naval architect Colin Moodie. The boat had a leeboard and a starboard rudder. Raw wool grease was spread over the leather hides which were stitched with flax. Alum-dressed thongs with tallow held together structural elements of the boat. This design reflected the type of vessel that Brendan used and showed that all aspects of Brendan's voyage could be replicated.

Chapter 7

BRITTANY, EUROPEAN RIVERS AND THE MEDITERRANEAN

The winds raise their blasts, the dread rain works its woe,
But men's ready strength conquers and routs the storm.

From the Rowing Song of Columbanus

Gaul

The whole of the coastline from the Loire estuary at St Nazaire to Mont St Michel at the base of the Cherbourg Peninsula was a regular sea highway for the Celtic saints from the fourth to seventh centuries, many of whom were born or educated in southern Wales.

The rugged granite cliffs and rocky shores of north-western Brittany are similar to those of Cornwall, and present a dangerous coastline to mariners. While there are many safe and sheltered inlets and estuaries, the difficulty for the master of the ship would be to find the entrance to these havens, which, from the deck of a small ship buffeted by waves in heavy weather, might appear to be little more than a dark cleft in a rough wall of rock and boulders surrounded by a cauldron of heaving white foam. The tidal range of up to twelve metres results in ferocious tide races of up to six knots around the headlands of Brittany and the Channel Isles, which would be impossible for any ship powered by sails or oars to make headway against. Passage plans therefore had to be timed to take account of the direction of the tidal streams. The voyage between the south-western shores of Britain and northern Brittany was also over seas exposed to the prevailing southwesterly gales of summer and northwesterlies of winter.

The tidal streams of the western approaches to Britain, Ireland and Brittany show such distinct patterns of the flood and ebb tides that it is easily seen how a knowledgeable shipmaster could use these streams to advantage.

The shortest crossing was across the English Channel from Boulogne to Dover òr Folkestone, a route favoured by the Romans and by Greek traders making for the Rhine, the Thames or rivers of the east coast of Britain. Even before the Roman fleet was withdrawn from Britain in the fifth century, Saxon pirates were reported in the channel, and after withdrawal of the Legions and the subsequent Saxon invasions and settlements of eastern England this was not a route that could be safely used by the Celts, particularly Christian saints and monks.

The Christian Celts of Gaul and Britain sought to avoid the pagan Saxons on land and at sea, and so were forced to undertake voyages far to the west of the English channel ports. The route from northern Brittany to south Wales or Cornwall would therefore be from established Brittany ports such as Treguier, perhaps via the Channel Islands of Jersey and Guernsey, and would then take a northwest heading to strike the Isles of Scilly and then the south coast of Cornwall, preferably east of the Lizard. There would then be only a short coastal passage with a favourable tide to take them to Golant in the Fal estuary for the overland route to Padstow and on to the south Wales coast.

Ships large enough and sturdy enough to cross from Cornwall to Brittany could also sail directly to south Wales or Ireland, with the Scillies again providing a useful port of refuge and suitable place to wait for a fair tide to sweep the vessel swiftly northwards into the approaches to St George's Channel or the Bristol Channel.

Saints of the south Wales province – links with Brittany

St Samson (485 – 565)

Voyages: Llanilltud Fawr – Ireland – Llanilltud Fawr –
Caldy Island – Padstow – St Kew, Southall –
Golant – Scilly Isles – Dol – Guernsey – Pental –
Normandy.

The patron saint of Brittany, St Samson, was a Welshman. He was taken as a young boy by his father (Amon, from Powys) and mother (from Gwent), to Illtud for his education at Llanilltud Fawr. Samson remained at Llanilltud Fawr and was ordained as a deacon and priest by Dyfrig, before he retired to Caldy Island, off the Pembrokeshire coast near Tenby. Whilst at Caldy he was ordained abbot and bishop, apparently with reluctance on his part, which may account for his leaving to live as a hermit on the banks of the river Severn. He then threw himself vigorously into his missionary work along the southern Wales coastal area, and also visited Ireland to reform a monastery there. In Ireland he purchased a chariot to carry his books and a coracle. He reputedly sailed in the coracle back to west Wales, then put the boat on the chariot and hired a horse to haul it to the south Welsh coast over the trans-peninsula route to Illtud's monastery. Once there the chariot was placed on the boat for the voyage to Padstow in Cornwall. From Padstow he then rode and voyaged on to Brittany, again using his boat and chariot. This was an innovative approach to travel over land and sea, but whilst the use of a chariot and a boat may well have been essential to Samson, it is unlikely that the size of vessel required for voyaging over the Irish Sea or from Cornwall to Brittany could be conveniently accommodated on a chariot.

Despite Samson's early work in Wales he is only associated with a few locations, such as Carreg Samson at Aberdaron, Caldy Island, Abercastell in Pembrokeshire, and Llanilltud Fawr. His legacy is however widely known on the other side of the Bristol Channel, in Cornwall, where he journeyed for some considerable time, attracting many converts and disciples. In Cornwall, Samson's route can be traced – it includes Padstow, St Kew, Southill and Golant. It is interesting to note that Padstow on the estuary of the river Camel on Cornwall's north coast, and Golant on the Fal estuary of Cornwall's south coast, are at the respective ends of the overland passage used by travellers wishing to avoid the dangerous sea journey around Lands End.

Samson was clearly at ease with sea travel, for in the course of his missionary work he undertook voyages to the Channel Isles, where a Guernsey town is named after him, and also to the Scilly Isles.

The Isles of Scilly are composed of forty-eight islands (some geographers state the number to be fifty, depending on how an 'island' is defined), although only five are inhabited today, these being St Mary's, St Agnes, St Martin's, Tresco and Bryher. The islands cover an area approximately ten miles by seven miles, and lie twenty to thirty miles west southwest of Lands End.

The Isles can be exposed to the Atlantic swell and unpredictable, fast changing weather. The Shell Channel Pilot, a modern pilot book for yachtsmen, states that 'half sea, half land, the Isles of Scilly lie out in the ocean, a paradise for sailors in fair weather, when the breezes are moderate, but a place for the stranger to avoid when the spume rises over the rocks and the gales blow hard'. It is clearly a place only for experienced navigators and soundly constructed ships. Both Samson and Martin of Tours are known to have carried out missionary work on the Scillies, and both have islands named after them to bear witness to their work.

Samson is thus honoured with an uninhabited island that lies to the south-west of Tresco. There is also Samson Hill, a prominent round hill on Bryher Island, which is used as a navigational mark for small vessels approaching the islands from the southeast. A welcoming beacon such as this is a fitting tribute to a sixth-century saint.

However, Samson's major pastoral and evangelical work was in Brittany, where he founded a monastery at Dol; he also founded a monastery at Pental in Normandy. He maintained his contacts with other Welsh monks, many of whom were also most active in the monastic life of Brittany.

Samson remained in Brittany where he attained a powerful position within the administrative, political and ecclesiastical concerns of Gaul as indicated by his signature of 'Samson Peccator Epscopus' – a senior ecclesiastical position – on the Acts of the Council of Paris of 557. Samson died in Brittany in 566.

St Teilo (sixth century)

Voyages: Penally – south-western Wales – Llanilltud Fawr – Cornwall – Dol – Brittany – south-eastern Wales.

As discussed in Chapter 5, Teilo was, like Samson, a pupil of Illtud during this time. A close relationship was formed between Teilo and Samson at Llanilltud Fawr, and so it was natural for Teilo to have sought refuge with Samson in 549, when he hurriedly left Cornwall to avoid the yellow plague epidemic. Teilo remained in Brittany for seven or eight years, but as he is also known to have visited Jerusalem it is likely that journey was made during this time.

St Illtud (475 – 525)

Voyages: southern Wales – Brittany – southern Wales

Both Samson and Teilo would have long known of the nature of Christian life in Brittany, for their former mentor and teacher, Illtud, had himself been active in the region as indicated by churches dedicated to him in Leon, Treguier and Vannes.

Illtud is associated with Germanus of Auxerre, who consulted with him when he was in Britain, so it is easily seen how the network and interchange between the Christians of Brittany and Wales was formed and nurtured.

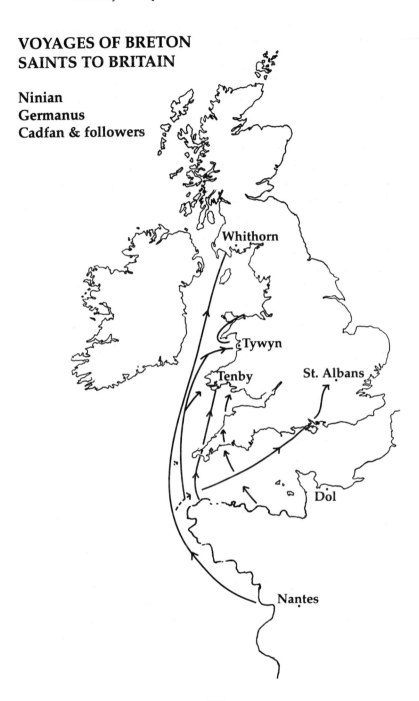

VOYAGES OF BRETON
SAINTS TO BRITAIN

Ninian
Germanus
Cadfan & followers

Whithorn

Tywyn

Tenby

St. Albans

Dol

Nantes

Located on the northern Brittany coast, Treguier offers excellent shelter, shielded as it is by the high wooded banks of the estuary of the river Jaudy. Treguier is today a charming town with its ancient cathedral on a hill overlooking the river. Illtud is acclaimed here, and this is likely to have been the destination of his fleet of cargo ships that carried grain from southern Wales to relieve the famine that had struck the settlement of northern Brittany.

Illtud is also known to have had links with Leon, further to the west of Treguier; Poullon near Dournanez, and Brieuc of northern Brittany, as well as Vannes located within the Golf de Morbihan of southern Brittany.

Gildas, another of Illtud's famous pupils, is also venerated in this area. Some of his writing is so critical of British kings and princes that it is unlikely that he would have produced this work while living in Britain, and it is believed to have originated towards the end of his life when he lived on the Isle du Rhus (St Gildas de Rhus) at the southern entrance to the Golf de Morbihan. This is virtually an inland sea of about fifty square miles. Only a few miles inland is the settlement of St Gildas le Bain and, back on the coast, the mariner approaching the mouth of the Loire will look for Point de St Gildas.

European rivers

While the sea provided the highway between countries for traders, soldiers, migrants and missionaries, the large rivers enabled them to cross those countries or penetrate far inland. The European river routes were extensively used by the Celtic saints.

Within the British Isles the location of monasteries and major ecclesiastical centres along the rivers of Ireland, Wales, Cornwall and Scotland show how important those rivers were for native missionaries and also for those arriving from mainland Europe and the Middle East. In Wales there is a preponderance of churches along the Severn, Wye, Usk, Teifi, Tawe and Tywi rivers of southern Wales, and the Dee and

Conwy rivers of northern Wales. Ireland has its important sites on the Shannon, Slaney, Suir and Lee rivers, while Scotland's Solway Firth and the Clyde are also significant. In Cornwall the Camel and the Fal were used by the saints not only to gain access to the interior of the peninsula for their missionary work, but also to facilitate the overland connection from the Bristol Channel to the south Cornwall coast, particularly to St Michael's Mount, as a leg of the western sea route to the continent.

On reaching mainland Europe, the huge highways of the Rhine, Rhône, Seine, Loire, Yonne, Marne and Garonne rivers allowed travellers to penetrate far into the continent. All these routes were used by traders, and in particular by the tin traders who voyaged to Britain from Mediterranean lands, and used the major European rivers to avoid the perilous offshore voyage down the Atlantic seaboard and the passage through the Strait of Gibraltar.

All these waterways were part of the network of well-established trade routes. The Garonne in south-western France was of major importance for the development of Britain, because it had been used since Bronze Age times by Greek and Minoan traders needing to access northwest Europe without having to make the long voyage through the Strait of Gibraltar and out into the Atlantic. A further alternative route was offered by entering the Rhône near the Mediterranean port of Cannes, to link over the watershed to the Rhine or Seine and eventually reach the channel ports. The Celtic saints would have been more familiar with the Garonne route to the Mediterranean for it was safer and more direct, but were also comfortable with the Loire and Yonne routes.

As already indicated, most Brythonic saints, particularly the Welsh, tended to work among their fellow Celts, but the Irish worked amongst the Saxons, Jutes and other pagan Germanic tribes in Britain and Europe, founding teaching monasteries wherever they could. An indication of their success is clearly recorded by the number of major locations in Europe where monasteries or communities were founded by Irish saints. The use of the western seaways and peninsula routes, such as Bordeaux to Narbonne, and the use of the European river system by entry at ports such as Nantes, Jumieges, are confirmed by the religious settlements they founded in those areas.

Major European sites in France, Germany, Austria, Switzerland and Italy may be summarised as:

France: River Gironde - Bordeaux, Moutier, Lure
       River Aude - Narbonne, St Ursainne
       River Loire - Nantes, Angers, Tours, Junigris, Meoux
       River Yonne - Auxerre, Jouarre, Rebais, Beze, Luxeuil, Leuconnais

Germany: Wurzburg, Sackingen
Austria: Salzburg
Italy: Bobbio
Switzerland: St Gall

As well as evangelical missions into Europe from the British Isles there were also missions from continental Europe to Britain – for example Germanus, Ninian and Cadog.

St Germanus (378-448)

Voyages: Auxerre – River Yonne – Brittany – Boulogne – Folkestone – Thames – St Germans, Cornwall – St Albans (Verulamium) – Brittany – Ravenna.

Germanus built a monastery on the banks of the river Yonne, facing the cathedral built within the fourth-century city walls. He was sent to Britain with Lupus of Troyes for a conference at Verulamium (St Albans) and he re-visited Britain in 447 to deal with a challenge to the Roman Church by the alleged heretical teachings of the Welsh monk Pelagius. While in Britain Germanus was also called on to direct British forces in battle against a combination of Picts and Saxon armies, indicating that, like many other monks of the post-Roman period, he had the benefit of a military

210

MAJOR EUROPEAN MONASTIC CENTRES
FOUNDED BY IRISH AND WELSH SAINTS

upbringing. The following year he was back in continental Europe, at Ravenna, pleading the case of Bretons with the Emperor. Gemanus was a major figure in the early Christian church in Britain: the Cornish town of St Germans is named after him, and fifteen ancient English churches are also dedicated to him.

Columbanus (543-615)

Voyages: Bangor – Cornwall – St Malo – Annegray, Burgundy – Luxeuil – Nantes – Biscay – Nantes – Neustria – Metz – Mainz – Rhine and tributaries Aar and Limmat to Arbon – Bregenz (Lake Constance) – Bobbio, Italy (between Milan and Genoa)

Columbanus was the most famous and most experienced of the monks who navigated along the European waterways. He was born on the Carlow-Wexford border, the son of a noble family, the Royal House of Leinster. He was a contemporary of such prominent saints as David, Columba and Kentigern. When he was seventeen he became a monk on the advice of a female hermit, after he admitted to carnal desires, and he trained as a student of Sinell on the island of Cleenish in Lough Erne, before entering St Comgall's monastery at Bangor, County Down. This monastery was formed under the strict rule of St Finnian, one of whose principles was a spartan diet consisting exclusively of water, vegetables and bread.

When Columbanus was fifty he sailed in a curragh out of Belfast Lough with twelve other monks with the objective of spreading Irish monastic rule throughout continental Europe. The party voyaged on the most direct route, making a stopover in Cornwall for supplies and then continuing to a landfall ten kilometres east of St Malo, which is commemorated by a granite cross in the village of Cancale

Columbanus had distinctive personal qualities and a rich personality. His achievements in the face of many difficulties – some brought about by his own actions – show him to have been a strong, energetic, forceful man: single-minded and courageous in tackling political and religious authority; influential and persuasive; occasionally austere; clearly a natural leader, but perhaps also a harsh leader and friend – his treatment of his loyal companion St Gall (who is discussed later) was not to his credit. He attracted many novices to his church, where as well as providing spiritual guidance he also taught astronomy, mathematics, geometry and handicrafts.

On reaching the Vosges area of Burgundy, Columbanus made his first permanent monastic settlement at Annegray, within the site of an old Roman fort given to him by the Frankish King Childebert. Here the group repaired a ruined Roman temple dedicated to the deity Diana, and re-dedicated it to Christ in honour of Martin of Tours.

When seeking a place of solitude away from the settlement, Columbanus is reputed to have discovered a cave that was already the lair of a bear. He asked the bear to leave, which it obligingly did – a tribute to the saint's persuasive charm. Later when surrounded by twelve hungry wolves Columbanus prayed and they went away.

Recruits and converts grew and Columbanus founded a new monastery in another old Roman fort at Luxeuil about twelve kilometres away. This was also highly successful. He founded yet another monastery in the area, at Fontaine, five kilometres to the north. The order followed a strict monastic rule, written by Columbanus, with a core of fasting, mortification, prayer, corporal punishment and repentance.

Columbanus taught Celtic Christian traditions, including the recognition of the Celtic Church date for Easter, and making a bishop subordinate to the abbot. These principles were politically dangerous. Many aspects of Columbanus' Irish traditions, particularly corporal punishment, the strict Rule and penitential practices, were considered too severe by the Roman Church. All of Columbanus' monasteries differed from the established Frankish customs in this respect and the divergent views resulted in friction with the established churches of the area. While Columbanus had the support of King Childebert he could overcome these objections and maintain his Celtic Irish Christian traditions, but on the king's death he lost his protector and was vulnerable to attack from the Archbishop of Lyons.

Columbanus refused to bless the illegitimate son of King Theuderic the 2nd, the King of Burgundy, and this not only incurred the wrath of the king but, more significantly, the king's mother, Brunhilde, who banished him from the kingdom. Columbanus and his followers were physically deported and taken under military escort to the port of Nantes. Here he was put on a trading ship sailing directly to Ireland. Columbanus was by then in his late sixties.

Not long into the voyage the ship encountered a succession of storms, which the captain interpreted as being a bad omen, and he therefore turned the ship around and returned to Nantes, where he disembarked Columbanus and his party. Columbanus still had powerful friends in France, and so took advantage of this turn of events to remain on the continent and travel upriver to Neustria, Metz, where at King Theudebert's court he met up with his Luxeuil monks.

Columbanus would not willingly be thwarted from installing his principles of Celtic Irish Christianity throughout Europe, and so, with his enlarged party of monks, set off on an immense voyage along the river systems and over the watersheds of Europe.

The party went on to Soissons, Paris, Meaux and Metz, from where they voyaged down the Moselle to Koblenz. They rowed up the Mainz. The next stage of their journey was the difficult passage up the Rhine and its tributaries, the Aar and then the Limmat: here they had to row against the current and step ashore to pull their boat by long lines when they encountered rapids too powerful to be able to make headway. This must have been the most arduous stage of the journey, and could only have been achieved by Columbanus' superb leadership. It was during this stage that his famous rowing song was composed to lift the spirits of his companions.

On reaching Basle they crossed over Lake Zurich to the former Roman town of Arbon on the southern shore of Lake Constance in Switzerland where they stayed for a while in the hospitality of the local priest, Father Willmar. They learned from Father Willmar of an old Roman fort at Bregenz, some twenty-five kilometres across Lake Constance in Austria. At Bregenz Columbanus hoped to settle, but he was still meeting fierce opposition from the established Roman churches, and his position again became untenable when he lost the protection of King Theudebert, who was defeated by Theuderic. The party also experienced antagonism from pagan groups in Bregenz, who were particularly incensed by the actions of one of the party, St Gall, when he removed many of their images and destroyed them or threw them into the lake. The safety of the group was at risk and, with regret for having to leave such a beautiful place, the epic journey resumed, continuing on foot over the Alps to Lombardy in northern Italy.

Four years after being deported by Brunhilde, Columbanus was preaching in Milan. He founded his final monastery at Bobbio in the foothills of the Apennines, dying there two years later in the year 613.

Despite his magnificent achievements Columbanus was not able to establish a lasting structure of monasteries based upon the Celtic Irish principles of Christianity, which, as ecclesiastical thinking developed, were considered to be too severe for the changing times. Nevertheless, Columbanus left a legacy of many learned manuscripts at Luxeuil and Bobbio, many letters to the Pope, numerous poems, and his famous rowing song, which is reproduced below and which was used to maintain the spirits of his companions on their arduous passages against the flow of some of the mightiest rivers in Europe.

Lo, cut in forests, the driven keel passes on the stream
Of twin horned Rhine, and glides as if anointed on the flood.

Ho, my men! Let ringing echo sound our Ho!
The winds raise their blasts, the dread rain works its woe,
But men's ready strength conquers and routes the storm.

Ho, my men! Let ringing echo sound our Ho!
For the clouds yield to endurance, and the storm yields,
Effort tames them all, unwearied toil conquers all things.

Ho, my men! Let ringing echo sound our Ho!
Bear, and preserve yourselves for favouring fortune,
Ye that have suffered worse, to these also God shall give an end.

Ho, my men! Let ringing echo sound our Ho!
Thus the hated foe deals as he wearies our hearts,
And by ill temptation shakes the inward hearts with rage.

Let your mind, my men, recalling Christ, sound Ho!

(Written by Columbanus on his trip up the Rhine,
translated by G. S. M. Walker)

St Gall (died 630)

Voyages: Bangor – Annegray, Burgundy – Luxeuil –
Nantes – Biscay – Nantes
Neustria – Metz – Mainz – Arbon – St Gallen

St Gall and Columbanus were companions for twenty years,
from the time that they raised the sail on their curragh to
leave Belfast Lough, until they parted under acrimonious
circumstances three years before Columbanus' death. St Gall
went on to outlive his former leader by another ten years. He
was a prominent member of the party and had the very
useful skill of being a good linguist. He spoke at least one of
the Germanic dialects, and in the library of St Gallen in
Switzerland is a Latin-German dictionary in Irish script
thought to be his. Gall was as dynamic in his actions as

THE RIVER VOYAGES OF
ST. COLUMBANUS & ST. GALL

Columbanus and when, on the shore of Lake Zurich, he came across a pagan German tribe worshipping the god Woden, he set fire to their temple and threw their sacrificial material into the lake. The pagan druid formulated a plot to murder Gall, and as a result Columbanus moved the group on to Arbon on the shore of Lake Constance.

Columbanus had learned of a deserted Roman fort across the lake at Bregenz in Austria Tyrol. Here the group found a church of St Aurelia which had once been a site of Christian worship but had become the pagan temple of a Germanic tribe. Gall was responsible for preaching to this tribe 'because he knew the Barbaric speech'. As part of his attempt to convert the tribe, Gall stripped the walls of symbols, smashed the pagan pottery and wooden images, and threw their bronze images into the lake. For a while there was danger of a violent response, but the monks eventually won over converts, re-dedicated the church and formed a settled community.

Gall was also a skilled fisherman; he repaired nets for the lakeside community and also kept a stock for visitors. However, some pagans had not been completely won over and they continued to work against the Christian group. They did not resort openly to violence but used a sophisticated legal and political campaign in an attempt to get the local ruler, Duke Gunzo, to expel the Christians for interfering with fishing and gaming rights. Two monks were also murdered when they went looking for a missing cow, and so the group moved on after only a year at Bregenz.

On the next stage of the journey Gall became ill and said he could not travel any further. Columbanus refused to accept his companion's illness as genuine, and thought Gall was simply being difficult or disloyal. He therefore left him behind, and also forbade him to ever celebrate mass again, which was a most harsh punishment.

Gall returned to the church of Father Willmar at Arbon where he was nursed back to full health. He remained at Arbon and, assisted by Father Willmar and two deacons

Magnoald and Theodore, he founded a hermitage. His influence grew in the region and when Gaudentius, Bishop of Constance died, Gall was proposed as bishop. He was promoted by Duke Gunzo, whose daughter had previously been healed by Gall. Gall declined the invitation on the grounds that he had been forbidden by his abbot (Columbanus) to take mass and also because he was not a native of the country, as was required by church law. He proposed another candidate, but agreed to read prayers in Latin at the service. He was also invited to lead the monastery at Luxueil but declined that honour as well.

Gall died in 630, the last of the group who had sailed out of Belfast Lough forty years earlier. Columbanus, who had dismissed Gall so unkindly, had repented of his behaviour and had bequeathed to him his bishop's staff when he died, as a gesture of reconciliation. Gall left a library of Irish manuscripts and an important ecclesiastical legacy, for around his hermitage grew a monastery, then a city, a diocese and finally the Canton of St Gallen.

The Mediterranean

The European rivers also linked northern Europe with the Mediterranean lands and provided alternative routes to the dangerous voyage down the western coast of Spain and Portugal for entry though the Strait of Gibraltar. Many of the Celtic saints followed these routes, particularly the Garonne passage, to reach Rome and Palestine.

The eastern Mediterranean is the location of one of the first recorded voyages made by a saint. Although not made by a Celtic saint, the voyage of St Paul from Lycia to Rome, which ended in a shipwreck on Malta, is an illuminating tale of the perils faced by early mariners. Paul's voyage, as a prisoner of the centurion Julius, was recorded by St Luke, who was a passenger on the same ship but who, unlike Paul, was not under arrest. The voyage was made on a merchant ship carrying grain which eventually ran ashore and was wrecked at St Paul's Bay, Malta, whilst taking a heavy battering in a storm.

Joseph of Arimathea was the first recorded missionary to Britain, and he followed the classic Greek tin-traders' route – not surprising because Joseph himself was a tin trader with business in northwestern Europe and had been making regular journeys to Britain before his own conversion to Christianity.

The concept of monks leaving the cloistered security of monasteries such as Bangor and Llanilltud Fawr and visiting Egypt, Palestine and Rome during the early middle ages is not easy for some present-day observers to imagine. Incredible although it may seem, they did undertake these challenging journeys, which pays testimony not only to the sophistication of society, knowledge and communication in the period, but also to the power of the faith of these remarkable men.

The Celtic saints undertook pilgrimage, missionary and study visits to the northern and eastern shores of the Mediterranean and, as in Britain, the sea was the only practical way to travel.

The eastern Mediterranean was the destination of Celtic saints such as Patrick, Ninian, Pelagius, Seiriol and others who made pilgrimages to Rome and to Jerusalem and other places in Palestine. One of the most distant destinations of the voyaging Celtic saints was Jerusalem and this was undertaken, most famously, by the Welsh saints Tysilio, Padarn and David, who would have experienced the dangers of all of the unpredictable and potentially fatal Mediterranean wind systems on their long journey when outward bound, and once again on their homeward voyage. The Welsh monk Pelagius was particularly well travelled throughout the Mediterranean. He visited Rome and Palestine many times, and also sought refuge for a while in Carthage, north Africa, when he was facing antagonism due to his alleged heretical views. He subsequently died in Palestine. In 825 the Irish monk Dicuil recorded that a voyaging monk by the name of Fidelis 'sailed down the Egyptian Nile and saw 'the Barns of Joseph' (the Pyramids) then crossed the Red Sea looking for parts of the Pharoah's chariots.

The name 'Mediterranean' nowadays generally conjures up a tranquil picture of a warm, blue sea with gentle waves lapping against a golden sandy beach. This vision is of a sea that is far kinder to mariners than the tides, squalls and fog of the cold grey waters of the northern latitudes. The reality, as shown by St Paul's experience, is often very different. It is true that the Mediterranean navigator does not have to worry about tides, which around Britain can result in the sea level falling by up to ten metres over a six-hour period, leaving boats stranded, or making channels too shallow to negotiate. Nor are there the strong tidal streams that can flow faster than the speed of a boat and so stop it in its track or even push it backwards, nor the ferocious tide races off rocky headlands, which can sweep a boat to its doom.

Neither was navigation in the Mediterranean a difficulty for the early medieval seafarers, for the maritime trade routes had been established for thousands of years. Navigation charts were available and these, combined with the knowledge of the kind of astro-navigation techniques as described in the Odyssey, and of the many islands and prominent headlands that enabled position fixes to be made, allowed Mediterranean voyages to be made with confidence.

But the Mediterranean of this period posed two major dangers to the mariner – pirates and weather. There were two ways of entering the Mediterranean for the Romano-Celtic travellers from Britain and Gaul: through the Strait of Gibraltar, or through the Gironde gap from Bayonne to Carcassonne. Entry through the Strait held the greatest risk of falling prey to pirates, because it required a course which at times was only twenty miles or so from the north African shore, before the vessel could start heading northwards for safer waters.

Rich cargoes were carried along the Mediterranean trade routes and these attracted pirates and plunderers who could find a ready market for wine, weapons, olive oil, precious metals, spices and slaves. The north African coast was a base for Moorish and Barbary pirates whose fast vessels could quickly overcome an unprotected merchantman who strayed too close to the Mediterranean's southern shore. Countless numbers of captured northern Europeans found themselves in the slave auctions of north Africa, where fair-skinned women and children were the 'white gold' of the economy, fetching premium prices. Men were put to work as oarsmen in galleys or as agricultural labourers. Even when mariners had passed through the Strait the risk of piracy was still a concern, for many islands of the Mediterranean provided relatively safe bases from which pirate ships could operate with impunity.

Travellers on ships passing through the Mediterranean would often be reminded of the proximity of these dangers when they detected the scents and dusty sand carried in the warm winds from the south. Low atmospheric pressure across the north African deserts produces a hot, dry, southerly wind from the desert called the Scirocco. (On the south coast of Spain this wind is called the Leveche.) The Scirocco carries sand and dust, and whilst it is hot and dry over the desert, it becomes moist as it blows over the sea, where it produces low cloud and severely reduces visibility as a consequence of the air-borne dust and moisture. The worrying images conjured up for the apprehensive seafarers by the scented smells of the Scirocco were therefore accentuated by poor visibility, which gave pirates an advantage in making an unseen approach on their prey.

By far the greatest danger arose from the weather. At first sight this may appear to be strange, for the Mediterranean is virtually a land-locked sea, apparently sheltered on all sides. This is where the problem arises – the Mediterranean is almost completely surrounded by mountains, but there are gaps through which the winds that enter are channelled into such ferocity and speed that they can wreak havoc on any exposed shipping. To the north, the Mediterranean is enclosed by the highest mountain ranges in Europe, represented by the Massif Central, the Alps, the Dolomites and the mountains of the Balkan states. To the south are the Atlas Mountains of Algeria and Morocco, and to the west is Cape St Vincent and the Atlantic-facing mountains of Spain and Portugal. In the east, behind the narrow coastal strip, are the towering mountain ranges of Turkey, Syria, the Lebanon and Sinai.

All of these mountain ranges deflect and so protect the Mediterranean from the atmospheric circulation that brings the prevailing Atlantic depressions which hammer against the shores of northwest Europe. But despite this protection, the Mediterranean does not entirely escape the effect of the global circulation of air masses. This is because the lower winds of the depressions force their way through the gaps in the mountain ranges, sometimes resulting in even greater severity. Atlantic depressions can also penetrate the Gironde gap between the Pyrenees and Massif Central to enter the Mediterranean in the Golfe de Lyon.

Voyagers such as St Patrick, who visited monasteries at the Isle de Lerins off the south coast of France and the Tyrrhenian Islands between Italy and Corsica, would have been particularly subject to the winds of the Golfe de Lyon.

Of even greater threat in this area are the northerly winds funnelled down the gaps created through the Massif Central and the Alps by the major river systems. The Rhône, which gave the traders and the Celtic saints access to the Mediterranean from northern Europe, also allows passage of the Mistral, which can blow down the valley to cause gale-force winds in the Golfe de Lyon. If the Mistral continues southwestwards along the Spanish coast it becomes the 'Levante' and if it is diverted to the east to reach Sardinia and Corsica and the Italian west coast it is known as the 'Libeccio'. These winds would have been feared by the shipmasters and by passengers such as Pelagius and Seiriol, heading for Rome, for although Mediterranean ships tended to be bigger than those of northern Europe, the effect on an unprepared sailing ship could be catastrophic.

From Perpignan to Genoa, Mistral winds will blow,

reaching their peak where the Rhône opens into the Camargue westwards from Marseille. The Mistral will flow through any gap in the mountains, descending down the valleys to the sea whenever there are winds from the north. The autumn, particularly October and November, has the lowest incidence – but gale force eight Mistrals are possible in spring and summer months.

The Strait of Gibraltar acts as a funnel, generating winds flowing east or west. When the Levante is blowing westwards out of the Mediterranean it creates a great plume of white cloud over the Rock of Gibraltar into the Atlantic, and is a warning to any approaching ship from northern Europe that it will face very strong winds on entering the Strait. Shelter beneath the most northern of the Pillars of Hercules would then be the only option for the voyaging saints. The equivalent east-flowing wind is the Vedaval, common in April but decreasing in summer, and while favourable for blowing the mariner into the Mediterranean it has the disadvantage of creating rough seas to the west of the Strait.

Despite all of the dangers the Celtic saints were familiar with voyaging to destinations on all parts of the Mediterranean shores and, most importantly, had the knowledge and ability to return safely to their communities in Wales, Scotland, Ireland and Cornwall.

Bibliography

Bamford & Marsh, W.P. *Celtic Christianity, Ecology and Holiness.* Edinburgh: Floris Books, 1986.

Berg, M. & Litvinoff, M. *Ancestors –The Origins of the People and Countries of Europe.* Oxford: Peter Lowe (Eurobook Ltd), 1992.

Bowen, E.G. *Settlements of the Celtic Saints in Wales.* Cardiff: University of Wales Press, 1954.

Saints, Seaways and Settlements. Cardiff: University of Wales Press, 1969.

Cunliffe, Tom. *The Shell Channel Pilot.* St Ives: Imray, Laurie, Norie & Wilson, 2000.

Davies, John. *A History of Wales.* London: Penguin, 1990.

Delap, Dana. *Celtic Saints.* Norwich: Pitkin Unichrome, 1995

D'Oliveira, B., Goulder, B., Lee-Elliott, E., (Eds) *Macmillan Reeds Nautical Almanac.* Emsworth: Nautical Data Ltd, 2002.

Ebenezer, L. *Aberystwyth.* Pwllheli: Llygad Gwalch Cyf, 2004.

Eluere, Christiane. *The Celts – First Masters of Europe.* London: Thames & Hudson Ltd, 1993.

Farmer, David. Hugh *The Oxford Dictionary of Saints.* Oxford: Oxford University Press, 2003.

Finch, Roger. *Sailing Craft of the British Isles.* London: Collins, 1976.

Fox, John. *Roman Coins and How to Collect Them.* London: Longman, 1983.

Friel, Ian. *Maritime History of Britain and Ireland.* London: The British Museum Press, 2003.

Griffiths, George. *A Cruising Guide to Northwest England & Wales.* St Ives: Imray, Laurie, Norie & Wilson, 1993.

Gruffydd, Elfed. *Llŷn.* Llanrwst: Gwasg Carreg Gwalch, 2003.

Hay, David & Hay, Joan. *No Star at the Pole.* Croydon: C Knight, 1972.

James, Simon. *Exploring the World of the Celts.* London: Thames & Hudson Ltd, 1993.

Jenkins, J.G. *Aberaeron and Ceinewydd.* Pwllheli: Llygad Gwalch Cyf, 2004.

Jones, Stephen. *The Language of the Genes.* London: Harper Collins, 1993.

Keller. *The Bible as History Revisited*. London: Bantam USA, 1983

Lawrence, Martin. *The Yachtsman's Pilot to the West Coast of Scotland*. St Ives: Imray, Laurie, Norie & Wilson, 1993.

Levy, David. *Skywatching*. London: Harper Collins, 1995.

Lloyd, I. *LPG*. Pwllheli: Llygad Gwalch Cyf, 2004.

Maredudd, O. & Jones, R.I. *Aberdyfi & Tywyn*. Pwllheli: Llygad Gwalch Cyf, 2004.

Marsden, Peter. *English Heritage book of Ships and Shipwrecks*. London: B.T.Batsford, 1997.

Moffat, Alistair. *The Sea Kingdoms*. London: Harper Collins, 2001.

Morgan, K.O. Ed. *The Oxford Popular History of Britain*. Oxford: Oxford University Press, 1993.

Mullins, Daniel. *Early Welsh Saints*. Llanrwst: Gwasg Carreg Gwalch, 2002.

Northern Ireland Tourist Board, Failte Ireland. *Ireland's Christian Heritage*, 2006.

O'Riordon, John J. *Early Irish Saints*. Dublin: Columba Press, 2001.

Oxenham, W. *The Welsh Origins of Scottish Place Names*. Llanwrst: Gwasg Carreg Gwalch, 2005.

Pennick, Nigel. *The Celtic Saints*. New York: Sterling Publication Co. Inc., 1997.

Roberts, I. *Abersoch and Llanbedrog*. Pwllheli: Llygad Gwalch Cyf, 2004.

Pwllheli. Pwllheli: Llygad Gwalch Cyf, 2004.

Roberts, Nyda. *The Bronze Age* – a Time of Change. Telford: Signal House Publications, 1994.

Russell, Bertrand. *History of Western Philosophy*. London: Routledge: 1961.

Severin, Tim. *The Brendan Voyage*. London: Hutchinson, 1978.

Spencer, R. *A Guide to the Saints of Wales and the West Country*. Lampeter: Llanerch Press, 1991.

Taylor, David. *Lundy and Irish Sea Pilot*. St Ives: Imray, Laurie, Norie & Wilson, 2001.

Tomes, John. *Blue Guide to Wales*. London: A&C Black, 1995.

Watney, John. *Celtic Wales*. Norwich: Pitkin Unichrome, 1997.

Watts, Alan. *The Weather*. Poole: Practical Boat Owner, 2005.

Illustrations

Photographic contributors:

Gordon Buchanan, Jannie Cariguel, Arthur Clarke, Peter Lyons, David Rainsbury, Alastair Scott, Alison Wood, Northern Ireland Tourist Board.

Index of Saints

Acknowledgements

Photographs by David Rainsbury:
    Pages 81, 82(A), 83(C), 88(A), 89
Photographs by Arthur Clarke:
    Page 86
Photographs by Tourisme Bretagne
    Pages 91, 92, 93(A)
Others: Gwasg Carreg Gwalch